Table of Contents

- **Chapter 1** 6
  - Mouth-Watering Apple Recipes 6
    - SPICY APPLE CRISP 6
    - RAISIN APPLE CRISP 7
    - CHOCOLATE APPLE CRISP 7
    - APPLE CAKE - 1 8
    - APPLE CAKE -2 8
    - APPLE FOOL 9
    - APPLE FLOAT 9
    - APPLE FRITTERS - 1 9
    - APPLE FRITTERS - 2 10
    - APPLE FRITTERS - 3 10
    - APPLE JELLY - 1 10
    - APPLE JELLY - 2 11
    - APPLE JELLY - 3 11
    - BOILED APPLE PUDDING 11
    - APPLE AND BROWN-BREAD PUDDING 12
    - BIRDS' NEST PUDDING 12
    - APPLE MELON PUDDING 12
    - APPLE SAGO 12
    - APPLE SAUCE - 1 13
    - APPLE SAUCE - 2 13
    - APPLE SAUCE - 3 13
    - CIDER APPLE SAUCE 13
    - OLD FASHIONED APPLE SAUCE 13
    - APPLE CREAM 14
- **Chapter 2:** 15
  - Salad Recipes 15
  - Collection of Easy to Follow Salad Recipes 15
    - CUCUMBER SALAD - 1 15
    - CUCUMBER SALAD - 2 16
    - CUCUMBER SALAD - 3 16
    - ONION SALAD - 1 16
    - ONION SALAD - 2 16
    - STUFFED TOMATO SALAD 17
    - TOMATO & STRING BEAN SALAD 17
    - BEET SALAD - 1 17
    - BEET SALAD - 2 18
    - BEET & BEAN SALAD 18
    - BEET AND CAULIFLOWER SALAD 18
    - STRING BEAN SALAD - 1 19
    - STRING BEAN SALAD - 2 19
    - STRING BEAN SALAD (FRENCH STYLE) 19
    - FRUIT SALAD DRESSING 20
    - MIXED FRUIT SALAD - 1 20
    - MIXED FRUIT SALAD - 2 21

- MIXED FRUIT SALAD - 3 21
- FRUIT SALAD (ICED) 21
- FRUIT AND NUT SALAD 21
- HUNGARIAN FRUIT SALAD 22
- RUSSIAN FRUIT SALAD 22
- SUMMER MIX FRUIT SALAD 22
- FILBERT & CHERRY SALAD 22
- DATE & WALNUT SALAD 23
- APPLE AND NUT SALAD 23
- APPLE, DATE & ORANGE SALAD 23
- ORANGE SALAD 24
- CALIFORNIA SALAD 24
- APPLE & CELERY SALAD 25

Chapter 3: 26
Deliciously Decadent Cheesecake Recipes 26
- Chocolate Raspberry Cheesecake 26
- Arizona Sunset Cheesecake 27
- Chocolate Chip Cheesecake Supreme 29
- Cappuccino Cheesecake 30
- Chocolate Mint Meringue Cheesecake 31
- Cherry Cheesecake 32
- Chocolate Turtle Cheesecake 33
- Chocolate Orange Supreme Cheesecake 34
- Cocoa-Nut Meringue Cheesecake 35
- Tempting Trifle Cheesecake 36

Chapter 4: 37
Recipes from South of the Border 37
- GRILLED CHICKEN QUESADILLAS 37
- Homemade Taco Sauce 37
- HOT & SPICY CHICKEN QUESADILLAS 38
- Hot Chile Sauce 39
- Hot Pickled Vegetables 39
- Huevos Rancheros 40
- JALAPENO CHICKEN FAJITAS 40
- Jalapeno Cream Sauce 41
- SUPPER NACHOS 41
- LA FOGATA'S GREEN CHICKEN ENCHILADAS 42
- LAZY ENCHILADAS 43
- Lentils with Chilies, Pork, and Fruit 44
- Lime Butter Sauce 45

Chapter 5: 46
120 Lip-Smacking Good Jam Recipes 46
- Fresh Strawberry Jam 46
- Ginger Peach Jam 46
- Gooseberry Jam 47
- Grandma Howard's Tomato Jam 47
- Ground Cherry Jam 48
- Instant Raspberry Cordial Jam 48
- Island Jam 49
- Pear & Ginger Jam 49

- Pear-Apple Jam 50
- Pineapple-Apricot Jam 51
- Quick Spiced Peach Jam 52
- Rose Hip Jam 53
- Rose Petal Jam 54
- Sherried Pear & Cranberry Jam 55
- Apricot, Orange & Almond Jam 56

Chapter 6: 57
The Ultimate Chicken Wing cookbook 57
- Barbecued Chicken Wings 57
- Beau's Sweet-Sour Chicken Wings 58
- BEAUJOLAIS-GLAZED CHICKEN WINGS 59
- Betty White's Chicken Wings Pacifica 60
- Blue Cheese Dip 60
- BLUE CORNMEAL CHICK WINGS 61
- Broiled Chicken Wings 62
- BRONZED CHICKEN WINGS WITH YOUNG GINGER 63
- Buffalo Chicken Wings 64
- BUFFALO CHICKEN WINGS #2 65
- BUFFALO CHICKEN WINGS #3 66
- BUFFALO CHICKEN WINGS #4 67
- BUFFALO CHICKEN WINGS #5 68
- BUFFALO CHICKEN WINGS #6 69
- BUFFALO CHICKEN WINGS W/ BLUE CHEESE DIPPING SAUCE 70
- BUFFALO CHICKEN WINGS WITH BLUE CHEESE DIPPING SAUCE 2 71
- Buffalo Wings, from Buffalo N.Y. 72
- CAJUN CHICKEN WINGS 72
- CAMPBELL'S HONEY MUSTARD WINGS 73
- Can't Get Enough Chicken Wings 74

Chapter 7: 75
Frozen Desert Recipes 75
- Simple Syrup: 75
- Custard Ice Cream Base: 75
- BANANA WALNUT 76
- BERRY, BERRY STRAWBERRY 76
- BLUEBERRY version 1 77
- BLUEBERRY version 2 77
- BROWN SUGAR PECAN 77
- BURNT CARAMEL 78
- BUTTER PECAN 78
- CARAMEL 79
- CARAMEL ALMOND 79
- CHERRY 80
- CHERRY BERRY 80
- CHOCOLATE version 1 81
- CHOCOLATE version 2 81
- CHOCOLATE version 3 82
- CHOCOLATE ALMOND 82
- CHOCOLATE ALMOND BUTTER 83
- CHOCOLATE BANANA 83

Chapter 1

Mouth-Watering Apple Recipes

SPICY APPLE CRISP

6 to 8 cooking apples
1 cup flour
1 1/2 cups brown sugar
3/4 cup butter
1/4 teaspoon ground cinnamon
1/4 teaspoon ground nutmeg
1 peel of one lemon
1 tablespoon fresh lemon juice

Peel, quarter and core cooking apples. Cut apple quarters into thin slices and place it in a bowl. Blend nutmeg and cinnamon then sprinkle over apples. Sprinkle with lemon rind. Add lemon juice and toss to blend. Arrange slices in a large baking dish. Make a mixture of sugar, flour and butter in a mixing bowl then put over apples, smoothing it over. Place the dish in the oven. If dish is very full, put a pan under the dish to catch spills. Bake at 370° for 60 minutes, until browned and apples are tender.

RAISIN APPLE CRISP

3 Apples
1/4 cup Raisins
1/4 cup Chopped nuts
1/8 cup Water
3/8 cup Brown sugar
1/8 teaspoon Cinnamon
1/2 tablespoon Lemon juice
2 tablespoon Flour
2 tablespoon margarine
1/8 teaspoon Salt

Wash, pare, core and slice apples thinly. Mix with raisins. Place in a greased casserole Add cinnamon, salt, lemon juice and water Work sugar, flour and margarine (fat) together to form crumb like consistency Spread over apple and raisin mixture Bake in 380 degree oven for at least 30 minutes.

CHOCOLATE APPLE CRISP

3 Apples, unpeeled if desired, chopped
1 1/2 cup flour
1 1/2 cup of uncooked Quick oats
1 cup of brown sugar
1 cup Pecans or walnuts, chopped
3/4 cup Butter
1/2 teaspoon Baking soda
1/4 teaspoon Salt
1 packet semi-sweet chocolate mini morsels, divided (12 oz)

Preheat the oven to 375 degrees F. In large bowl, combine flour, brown sugar, baking soda and salt. With 2 knives or pastry blender, cut in butter until mixture resembles fine crumbs. Stir in oats; press half of oat mixture into greased 13x9" baking pan. To remaining oat mixture, add Nestle Toll House semi-sweet chocolate mini morsels, apples and pecans; stir to combine. Sprinkle over base. Bake at least 35 minutes until lightly browned. Cool slightly; cut into squares.

APPLE CAKE - 1

6 oz. Allinson fine wheat meal
6 oz. white flour
4-1/2 butter
1 - egg
1-1/2 lbs. of apples
1 teaspoonful cinnamon
3 oz. castor sugar
and a little cold water

Rub the butter into the meal and flour, beat up the egg and add it, and as much cold water as is required to make a smooth paste; roll out the greater part of it 1/4 inch thick, and line a flat buttered tin with it. Pare, core, and cut the apples into thin divisions, arrange them in close rows on the paste point down, leaving 1 inch of edge uncovered; sift the sugar and cinnamon over the apples; roll out thinly the rest of the paste, cover the apples with it, turn up the edges of the bottom crust over the edges of the top crust, make 2 incisions in the crust, and bake the cake until brown in a moderately hot oven; when cold sift castor sugar over it, slip the cake off the tin, cut into pieces, and serve.

APPLE CAKE -2

1-1/2 cups flour
3 teaspoons Baking Powder
1/2 teaspoon salt
2 tablespoons shortening
1/2 cup milk
4 or 5 apples
1/2 cup sugar
1 teaspoon cinnamon

Sift together flour, baking powder and salt; add shortening and rub in very lightly; add milk slowly to make soft dough and mix. Place on floured board and roll out 1/2-inch thick. Put into shallow greased pan. Wash, pare, core and cut apples into sections; press them into dough, sprinkle with sugar and dust with cinnamon. Bake in moderate oven 30 minutes or until apples are tender and brown. Serve warm with milk or cream.

APPLE FOOL

2 lbs. of apples
1/2 lb. of dates]
3/4 pint of milk
1/4 pint of cream
6 cloves tied in muslin
and a little sugar.

Pare, core, and cut up the apples, stone the dates, and gently stew the fruit with a teacupful of water and the cloves until quite tender; when sufficiently cooked, remove the cloves, and rub the fruit through a sieve; gradually mix in the milk, which should be boiling, then the cream; serve cold with sponge-cake fingers.

APPLE FLOAT

12 apples, pared and cored
1 1/2 pound of sugar
1 large lemon
1 ounce of gelatin
and water as necessary

Put the apples on with water enough to cover them and let them stew until they look as if they would break; then take them out and put the sugar in the same water; let the syrup come to a boil, put in the apples and let them stew until done through and clear; then take them out, slice into the syrup one large lemon and add an ounce of gelatin dissolved in a pint of cold water. Let the whole mix well and come to a boil; then pour upon the apples. The syrup will congeal. It is to be eaten cold with cream.

APPLE FRITTERS - 1

3 good juicy cooking apples
3 eggs
6 oz. of Allinson fine wheat meal
1/2 pint of milk
and sugar to taste.

Pare and core the apples, and cut them into rounds 1/4 inch thick; make a batter with the milk,
meal, and the eggs well beaten, adding sugar to taste. Have a frying-pan ready on the fire with boiling oil, vege-butter, or butter, dip the apple slices into the batter and fry the fritters until golden brown; drain them on blotting paper, and keep them hot in the oven until all are done.

APPLE FRITTERS - 2

4 Eggs
four spoonfuls of fine flour
1/4 pound of sugar
Milk, Nutmeg and Salt as necessary

Take four eggs and beat them very well, put to them four spoonfuls of fine flour, a little milk, about a quarter of a pound of sugar, a little nutmeg and salt, so beat them very well together; you must not make it very thin, if you do it will not stick to the apple; take a middling apple and pare it, cut out the core, and cut the rest in round slices about the thickness of a shilling; (you may take out the core after you have cut it with your thimble) have ready a little lard in a stew-pan, or any other deep pan; then take your apple every slice single, and dip it into your bladder, let your lard be very hot, so drop them in; you must keep them turning whilst enough, and mind that they be not over brown; as you take them out lay them on a pewter dish before the fire whilst you have done; have a little white wine, butter and sugar for the sauce; grate over them a little loaf sugar, and serve them up.

APPLE FRITTERS - 3

Make a batter in the proportion of one cup sweet milk to two cups flour, a heaping teaspoonful of baking powder, two eggs beaten separately, one tablespoonful of sugar and a salt spoon of salt; heat the milk a little more than milk-warm, add it slowly to the beaten yolks and sugar; then add flour and whites of the eggs; stir all together and throw in thin slices of good sour apples, dipping the batter up over them; drop into boiling hot lard in large spoonfuls with pieces of apple in each, and fry to a light brown. Serve with maple syrup, or nice syrup made with clarified sugar.

APPLE JELLY - 1

Take many apples as may be required. 1 pint of water to each 1 lb. of apples. Wash and cut up the apples, and boil them in the water until tender; then pour them into a jelly bag and let drain well; take 1 lb. of loaf sugar to each pint of juice, and the juice of 1 lemon to each quart of liquid. Boil the liquid, skimming carefully, until the jelly sets when cold if a drop is tried on a plate. It may take from 2 hours to 3 hours in boiling.

APPLE JELLY - 2

Select apples that are rather tart and highly flavored; slice them without paring; place in a porcelain preserving kettle, cover with water, and let them cook slowly until the apples look red. Pour into a colander, drain off the juice, and let this run through a jelly-bag; return to the kettle, which must be carefully washed, and boil half an hour; measure it and allow to every pint of juice a pound of sugar and half the juice of a lemon; boil quickly for ten minutes. The juice of apples boiled in shallow vessels, without a particle of sugar, makes the most sparkling, delicious jelly imaginable. Red apples will give jelly the color and clearness of claret, while that from light fruit is like amber. Take the cider just as it is made, not allowing it to ferment at all, and, if possible; boil it in a pan, flat, very large and shallow.

APPLE JELLY - 3

Take twenty large ripe juicy pippins. Pare, core, and chop them to pieces. Put them into a jar with the yellow rind of four lemons, pared thin and cut into little bits Cover the jar closely, and set it into a pot of hot water Keep the water boiling hard all round it till the apples are dissolved, Then strain them through a jelly-bag, and mix with the liquid the juice of the lemons. To each pint of the mixed juice allow a pound of loaf-sugar. Put them into a porcelain kettle, and when the sugar is melted, set it on the fire, and boil and skim it for about twenty minutes, or till it becomes a thick jelly. Put it into tumblers, and cover it with double tissue paper nicely fitted to the inside of the top. The red or Siberian crab apple makes a delicious jelly, prepared in the above manner.

BOILED APPLE PUDDING

3 apples
3 eggs
1/4 pound of breadcrumbs
1 lemon
3 ounces sugar
3 ounces of currants
1/2 a wine-glassful of wine
nutmeg, butter and sugar as necessary

Pare, core and mince the apples and mix with the bread crumbs, nutmeg, grated sugar, currants; the juice of the lemon and half the rind grated. Beat the eggs well, moisten the mixture with these and beat all together, adding the wine last; put the pudding in a buttered mold, tie it down with a cloth; boil one hour and a half and serve with sweet sauce.

APPLE AND BROWN-BREAD PUDDING

Take a pint of brown bread crumbs, a pint bowl of chopped apples, mix; add two-thirds of a cupful of finely-chopped suet, a cupful of raisins, one egg, a tablespoonful of flour, half a teaspoonful of salt. Mix with half a pint of milk, and boil in buttered molds about two hours. Serve with sauce flavored with lemon.

BIRDS' NEST PUDDING

Core and peel eight apples, put in a dish, fill the places from which the cores have been taken with sugar and a little grated nutmeg; cover and bake. Beat the yolks of four eggs light, add two teacupfuls of flour, with three even teaspoonfuls of baking powder sifted with it, one pint of milk with a teaspoonful of salt; then add the whites of the eggs well beaten, pour over the apples and bake one hour in a moderate oven. Serve with sauce.

APPLE MELON PUDDING

1 lb. of Allinson breadcrumbs, 3 apples, 1-1/2 lbs. of melon, 12 cloves, 1/2 pint of milk, 1 oz. of butter, 3 eggs, sugar to taste. Peel and cut up the apples and melon, and stew the fruit 15 minutes, adding sugar and the cloves tied in muslin. Place a layer of breadcrumbs in a buttered dish, remove the cloves from the fruit, place a layer of fruit over the breadcrumbs, and so on until the dish is full, finishing with a layer of breadcrumbs; beat up the eggs, mix them with the milk, and pour the mixture over the pudding; spread the butter in bits over the top, and bake the pudding 1 hour.

APPLE SAGO

1-1/2 lbs. of apples
5 oz. of sago
Juice of a lemon
A teaspoonful of ground cinnamon
and sugar to taste.

Wash the sago and cook it in 1-1/2 pints of water, to which the cinnamon is added; meanwhile have the apples ready, pared, cored, and cut up; cook them in very little water, just enough to keep the apples from burning; when they are quite soft rub them through a sieve and mix them with the cooking sago, adding sugar and lemon juice; let all cook gently for a few minutes or until the sago is quite soft; put the mixture into a wetted mould, and turn out when cold.

APPLE SAUCE - 1

1 lb. of good cooking apples
Sugar to taste.

Pare, core, and cut in pieces the apples, cook them in a few spoonfuls of water to prevent them burning; when quite soft rub the apple through a sieve, and sweeten the sauce to taste. Rubbing the sauce through a sieve ensures the sauce being free from pieces should the apple not pulp evenly.

APPLE SAUCE - 2

When you wish to serve apple sauce with meat prepare it in this way:- Cook the apples until they are very tender, then stir them thoroughly so there will be no lumps at all; add the sugar and a little gelatin dissolved in warm water, a tablespoonful in a pint of sauce; pour the sauce into bowls, and when cold it will be stiff like jelly, and can be turned out on a plate.

APPLE SAUCE - 3

1 lb. of apples, 1 gill of water, 1-1/2 oz. of sugar (or more, according to taste), 1/2 a teaspoonful of mixed spice. Pare and core the apples, cut them up, and cook them with the water until quite mashed up, add sugar and spice. Rub the apples through a sieve, re-heat, and serve. Can also be served cold.

CIDER APPLE SAUCE

Boil four quarts of new cider until it is reduced to two quarts; then put into it enough pared and quartered apples to fill the kettle; let the whole stew over a moderate fire four hours; add cinnamon if liked. This sauce is very fine with almost any kind of meat.

OLD FASHIONED APPLE SAUCE

Pare and chop a dozen medium-sized apples, put them in a deep pudding-dish; sprinkle over them a heaping coffee cupful of sugar and one of water. Place them in the oven and bake slowly two hours or more, or until they are a deep red brown; quite as nice as preserves.

APPLE CREAM

6 large apples (coslings or any other apples that will be soft)
4 eggs
3/4-pound double-refined sugar
1-2 spoonful of rose water
And lemon-peel.

Take your apples and coddle them; when they are cold take out the pulp; then take the whites of four or five eggs, (leaving out the strains) three quarters of a pound of double-refined sugar beat and sifted, a spoonful or two of rose-water and grate in a little lemon-peel, so beat all
Together for an hour, whilst it be white, then lay it on a china dish, to serve it up.

Chapter 2:
Salad Recipes

Vegetable Salads:

CUCUMBER SALAD - 1

Besides serving plain slices of cucumber on a lettuce leaf, as may be done at any time, cucumbers may be used as an ingredient in the making of many salads.

3 medium-sized cucumbers
1 c. diced tomato
1/2 c. diced celery
Salad dressing
Lettuce
1 pimiento

Peel the cucumbers, cut them into halves, and with a small spoon scoop out the cucumbers in chunks, so that a boat-shaped piece of cucumber that is about 1/4 inch thick remains. Dice the pieces of cucumber which have been scooped from the center, and place the cucumber shells in ice water so as to make them crisp. Mix the diced tomato, celery, and cucumber together, and just before serving drain them carefully so that no liquid remains. Mix with salad dressing, wipe the cucumber shells dry, fill them with the salad mixture, and place on salad plates garnished with lettuce leaves. Cut the pimiento into thin strips, and place three or four strips diagonally across the cucumber. Sufficient to Serve Six

CUCUMBER SALAD - 2

Pare thickly, from end to end, and lay in ice-water one hour; wipe them, slice thin, and slice an onion equally thin. Strew salt over them, shake up a few times, cover and let remain in this brine for another hour. Then squeeze or press out every drop of water which has been extracted from the cucumbers. Put into a salad bowl, sprinkle with white pepper and scatter bits of parsley over them; add enough vinegar to cover. You may slice up an equal quantity of white or red radishes and mix with this salad.

CUCUMBER SALAD - 3

Peel and slice a cucumber, mix together 1/2 a teaspoonful of salt, 1/4 of a teaspoonful of white pepper, and 2 tablespoonfuls of olive oil, stir it well together, then add very gradually 1 tablespoonful of vinegar, stirring it all the time. Put the sliced cucumber into a salad dish, and garnish it with nasturtium leaves and flowers.

ONION SALAD - 1

To persons who are fond of the flavor of onions, the salad given in the accompanying recipe is very agreeable, but it is a wise plan not to serve onions or salads containing onions unless every one who is served is certain to enjoy them. When a salad is made from onions, a mild onion should be selected.

3 onions
French dressing
Parsley
Lettuce

Peel the onions and slice them into thin slices. Chop the parsley and add it to 1 or 2 tablespoonfuls of French dressing. Use comparatively coarse leaves of lettuce and shred them. Arrange the slices of onion on a bed of the shredded lettuce, pour the French dressing with the parsley over all, and serve. Sufficient to Serve Six.

ONION SALAD - 2

1 large boiled onion (Spanish), 3 large boiled potatoes, 1 teaspoonful of parsley, pepper and salt to taste, juice of 1 lemon, 2 or 3 tablespoonfuls of olive oil. Slice the onion and potatoes when quite cold, mix well together with the parsley and pepper and salt; add the
lemon juice and oil, and mix well once more.

STUFFED TOMATO SALAD

An attractive salad in which vegetables of almost any kind, fresh or canned, may be used to
advantage is the stuffed tomato salad. Medium-sized, well-ripened tomatoes are best to select. The vegetables that may be used for the stuffing are celery, radishes, onions, cucumbers, cooked asparagus, green peas, and string beans. Any one or any desirable combination of these vegetables will make a satisfactory filling.

6 medium-sized tomatoes
French dressing
1 1/2 c. diced vegetables
Mayonnaise dressing

Cut out the stem and blossom ends of the tomatoes and hollow out the center so as to leave a shell. Dice the contents of the tomatoes and mix with the other diced vegetables. Marinate the diced vegetables with French dressing and put into the tomato shells, heaping each one as shown. Place on lettuce leaves and serve with mayonnaise.

TOMATO & STRING BEAN SALAD

Besides being appetizing in flavor and appearance, tomato and string-bean salad has the advantage over some salads in that it can be made of either fresh or canned vegetables. For the salad here shown, tomatoes and beans canned by the cold-pack method were used. If it is desired to duplicate this salad, place a canned tomato or a peeled fresh tomato in the center of a plate garnished with lettuce and around it place several piles of three or four canned or freshly cooked beans. Serve with French dressing or any other desired salad dressing.

BEET SALAD - 1

Cold boiled or baked beets, chopped quite fine, but not minced, make a nice salad when served with a dressing of lemon juice and whipped cream in the proportion of three tablespoonfuls of lemon juice to one half cup of whipped cream, and salt if desired.

BEET SALAD - 2

Chop equal parts of boiled beets and fresh young cabbage. Mix thoroughly, add salt to taste, a few tablespoonfuls of sugar, and cover with diluted lemon juice. Equal quantities of cold boiled beets and cold boiled potatoes, chopped fine, thoroughly mixed, and served with a dressing of lemon juice and whipped cream, make a palatable salad.

BEET & BEAN SALAD

An excellent winter salad and one that may be made from canned or left-over vegetables is beet & bean salad. If string beans happen to be left over or only part of a can remains, they
may be combined with beets that are canned or freshly cooked for the purpose. This salad should be carefully combined just before serving.

1 c. string beans
Lettuce
1 c. beets
Salad dressing

Cut the string beans into half-inch lengths and cut the beets into half-inch dice. Season each well with salt and pepper. Just before serving, garnish salad plates with lettuce, combine the two vegetables, and place in a heap on a lettuce leaf. Pour French dressing or any other salad dressing desired over them, but do not mix the salad dressing with the vegetables. Sufficient to Serve Four.

BEET AND CAULIFLOWER SALAD

Take some thin slices of cooked beets, some cold cooked potatoes, some cold cooked cauliflower, and a little chopped parsley. Pour over the following dressing and add salt and pepper to taste:

Put one level teaspoon of mustard, one teaspoon anchovy sauce, one tablespoon of milk or cream, and one dessertspoon of vinegar. Mix the mustard with the anchovy, then add the milk, and lastly the vinegar.

STRING BEAN SALAD - 1

Either string or wax beans may be used for string bean salad and they may be cooked freshly for the purpose or be home canned or commercially canned beans. To make this salad, place a neat pile of beans on a lettuce leaf resting on a plate and moisten with a few drops of vinegar or lemon juice. Serve with mayonnaise or cooked salad dressing. If desired, the beans may be cut into inch lengths and mixed with the dressing, but this does not make so attractive a salad.

STRING BEAN SALAD - 2

String and remove the ends from one quart of beans. Cut into short lengths. Cover with boiling water, add one level tablespoon of wilt and cook until tender, but not soft. Drain and save one cup of the liquor. Cream one tablespoon of flour with two tablespoons of butter. Pour the liquid over the flour and butter, stirring constantly. Cook this sauce for five minutes, remove from stove and stir in two tablespoons of strained lemon juice. Pour this over the beans and serve.

STRING BEAN SALAD (FRENCH STYLE)

String the beans and boil them whole; when boiled tender and they have become cold, slice them lengthwise, cutting each bean into four long slices; season them an hour or two before serving, with a marinade of a little pepper, salt, and three spoonfuls of vinegar to one spoonful of oil. Just before serving, drain from them any drops of superfluous liquid that may have collected and carefully mix them with a French Salad dressing. This makes a delicious salad.

Fruit Salads:

FRUIT SALAD DRESSING

Various dressings may be served with fruit salad, and usually the one selected depends on the preference of those to whom it is served. However, an excellent dressing for salad of this kind and one that most persons find delicious is made from fruit juices thickened by means of eggs. Whenever a recipe in this Section calls for a fruit salad dressing, this is the one that is intended.

1/2 c. pineapple, peach, or pear juice
1/2 c. orange juice
1/4 c. lemon juice
1/4 c. sugar
2 eggs

Mix the fruit juices, add the sugar, beat the eggs slightly, and add them. Put the whole into a double boiler and cook until the mixture begins to thicken. Remove from the fire and beat for a few seconds with a rotary egg beater. Cool and serve.

MIXED FRUIT SALAD - 1

The combination of fruits given in the accompanying recipe makes a very good salad, but it need not be adhered to strictly. If one or more of the fruits is not in supply, it may be omitted and some other used. In case canned pineapple is used for the salad, the juice from the fruit may be utilized in making a fruit salad dressing.

1 grapefruit
2 oranges
1 banana
2 apples
2 slices pineapple
Salad dressing
Lettuce

Prepare the grapefruit and oranges according to the directions previously given. Slice the banana crosswise into 1/4-inch slices and cut each slice into four sections. Dice the apples and cut the pineapple in narrow wedge-shaped pieces. Mix the fruit just before serving. Add the salad dressing, which may be fruit-salad dressing, French dressing, or some other desirable salad dressing, by mixing it with the fruit or merely pouring it over the top. Serve on salad plates garnished with lettuce leaves. Place a maraschino cherry on top. Sufficient to Serve Six.

MIXED FRUIT SALAD - 2

Take sweet, ripe oranges, apples, bananas, and grapes. Peel the oranges, quarter them, and remove skin and pips. Peel and core the apples and cut into thin slices. Wash and dry the grapes, and remove from stalks. Skin and slice the bananas. Put the prepared fruit into a glass dish in alternate layers. Squeeze the juice from 2 sweet oranges and pour over the salad. Any other fresh fruit in season may be used for this salad. Castor sugar may be sprinkled over if desired, and cream used in place of the juice. Grated nuts are also a welcome addition.

MIXED FRUIT SALAD - 3

Slice one pineapple, three oranges, and three bananas. Pour over it a French mayonnaise, put on lettuce leaves and serve at once. For those who do not care for the mayonnaise, make a syrup of one cup of sugar and one-half cup of water, boil until thick, add juice of lemon, let slightly cool, then pour over fruit. Let stand on ice for one hour. Another nice dressing is one cup of claret, one-half cup of sugar, and piece of lemon. Always use lemon juice in preference to vinegar in fruit salads. All fruits that go well together may be mixed. This is served just before desert.

FRUIT SALAD (ICED)

Make one quart of lemon or orange water ice and stand it aside for at least one or two hours to ripen. Make a fruit salad from stemmed strawberries, sliced bananas cut into tiny bits, a few very ripe cherries, a grated pineapple if you have it, and the pulp of four or five oranges. After the water ice is frozen rather hard, pack it in a border mold, put on the lid or cover and bind the seam with a strip of muslin dipped in paraffin or suet, and repack to freeze for three or four hours. Sweeten the fruit combination, if you like, add a tablespoonful or two of brandy and sherry, and stand this on the ice until very cold. At serving time, turn the mold
of water ice on to a round compote dish, quickly fill the centre with fruit salad, garnish the outside with fresh roses or violets, and send at once to the table.

FRUIT AND NUT SALAD

Slice two bananas, two oranges and mix them with one-half cup of English walnuts and the juice of one-half lemon with French dressing. Serve on lettuce leaves.

HUNGARIAN FRUIT SALAD

Mix together equal parts of banana, orange, pineapple, grapefruit and one-half cup of chopped nuts. Marinate with French dressing. Fill apple or orange skins with mixture. Arrange on a bed of watercress or lettuce leaves. Sprinkle with paprika.

RUSSIAN FRUIT SALAD

Peel and pit some peaches, cut in slices and add as much sliced pineapple, some apricots, strawberries and raspberries, put these in a dish. Prepare a syrup of juice of two lemons, two oranges, one cup of water and one pound sugar, a half teaspoon of powdered cinnamon, grated rind of lemon, add one cup red wine and a half glass of rum. Boil this syrup for five minutes, then pour over the fruit, tossing the fruit from time to time until cool. Place on ice and serve cold.

SUMMER MIX FRUIT SALAD

Any agreeable combination of fruits which may be obtained during the same season will be suitable for summer mix salad. The combination given in the accompanying recipe includes strawberries, pineapple, and cherries. However, pineapple and cherries may be used alone, or strawberries and pineapple may be used without the cherries, or red raspberries may be used to garnish such a salad.

3/4 c. strawberries, cut into halves
3/4 c. pineapple, cut into dice
3/4 c. sweet cherries, seeded
Lettuce
Fruit-salad dressing

Prepare the fruits just before serving. Put them together, place on salad plates garnished with lettuce, and serve with the fruit-salad dressing.

FILBERT & CHERRY SALAD

If something different in the way of salad is desired, cherries that have been seeded and then filled with filberts will prove a delightful change. With this salad, any salad dressing may be served, but fruit-salad dressing makes it especially delicious.

DATE & WALNUT SALAD

Persons who are fond of dates will find a salad made of dates and walnuts very palatable. In addition, such a salad is high in food value. Select firm whole dates, wash, and dry between clean towels. Cut a slit in the side of each date and remove the seed. Place half an walnut meat inside and press the date together. Garnish salad plates with lettuce and serve five or six of the dates in a star shape for each serving. In the center, pour a spoonful or two of cream salad dressing, boiled salad dressing, or any other dressing that may be desired.

APPLE AND NUT SALAD

4 tart apples
1 cupful of pecan meats
24 blanched almonds
2 sweet Spanish peppers

The rule for French dressing

Peel the apples, cut them into dice, squeeze over the juice of one or two lemons, and stand them aside until wanted. The lemon juice will prevent discoloration. Chop the nuts. At serving time line the salad bowl with a layer of chopped celery or cabbage or lettuce leaves, then a layer of apples, nuts, celery, apples and nuts. Baste with the French dressing, and, if you have them, garnish with the sweet peppers cut into strips, and use at once.

APPLE, DATE & ORANGE SALAD

The combination of fruits required by the accompanying recipe is an easy one to procure in the winter time. Apple and date salad is a combination much liked, but unless it is served with a rather sour dressing, it is found to be too bland and sweet for most persons. The addition of the orange gives just the acid touch that is necessary to relieve this monotonous sweetness.

1 c. diced apples Lettuce
3/4 c. dates, seeded Salad dressing
2 oranges
Lettuce
Salad Dressing

Peel the apples and dice them into fine pieces. Wash the dates, remove the seeds, and cut each date into six or eight pieces. Prepare the oranges as directed for preparing oranges for salad, and cut each section into two or three pieces. Just before serving, mix the fruits carefully so as not to make the salad look mushy, pile in a neat heap on garnished salad plates, and serve with any desired dressing. Sufficient to Serve Six

ORANGE SALAD

INGREDIENTS: 6 oranges, 1/4 lb. of muscatel raisins, 2 oz. of pounded sugar, 4 tablespoonfuls of brandy.

Peel 5 of the oranges; divide them into slices without breaking the pulp, and arrange them on a glass dish. Stone the raisins, mix them with the sugar and brandy, and mingle them with the oranges. Squeeze the juice of the other orange over the whole, and the dish is ready for table. A little pounded spice may be put in when the flavour is liked; but this ingredient must be added very sparingly.

CALIFORNIA SALAD

During the months in which California grapes can be found in the market, a very delicious salad can be made by combining them with grapefruit and oranges. Either Malaga or Tokay grapes may be used.

1-1/2 c. grapes
2 oranges Salad
1 grapefruit
Lettuce
Salad Dressing

Prepare the grapes by washing them in cold water, cutting them into halves, and removing the seeds. Remove the sections from the oranges and grapefruit in the way previously directed, and cut each section into three or four pieces. Mix the fruits and drain carefully so that they contain no juice or liquid. Pile in a heap on salad plates garnished with lettuce and serve with any desired dressing.

APPLE & CELERY SALAD

If an excellent winter salad is desired, apple and celery salad should be selected, for both celery and apples are best during the winter months. As they are very similar in color, they are not especially appetizing in appearance when combined for a salad, but they make a very popular combination with most persons.

1 c. diced apples
Boiled salad dressing
1 c. diced celery
Lettuce

Prepare the apples and celery as short a time before serving as possible, but if it is necessary that the apples stand for any length of time, sprinkle them with a little lemon juice and water to keep them from turning brown. Just before serving, mix them with the salad dressing. Place on salad plates garnished with lettuce and serve. Sufficient to Serve Four.

Chapter 3:

Deliciously Decadent Cheesecake Recipes

Chocolate Raspberry Cheesecake

1 1/2 c Creme-filled Cookie Crumbs *
2 tb Margarine, Melted
32 oz Cream Cheese, Softened
1 1/4 c Sugar
3 ea Large Eggs
1 c Sour Cream
1 ts Vanilla
6 oz Semi-sweet Chocolate Chips**
1/3 c Strained Raspberry Preserves
6 oz Semi-sweet Chocolate Chips
1/4 c Whipping Cream

Cookie crumbs should come from 18 Cream Filled Cookies that have been finely crushed. This 6 ozs of Chocolate chips should be melted and cooled slightly .
Combine crumbs and margarine; press onto bottom of 9-inch springform pan. Combine 24 ozs of cream cheese and sugar, mixing at medium speed on electric mixer until well blended. Add eggs, one at a time, beating well after each addition. Blend in sour cream and vanilla; pour over crust. Combine remaining 8 ozs cream cheese and melted chocolate, mixing at medium speed on eletric mixer until well blended. Add Red Raspberry preserves; mix well. Drop rounded measuring tablespoonsfuls of chocolate cream cheese batter over plain cream cheese batter, do not swirl. Bake at 325 degrees F., 1 hour and 25 minutes. Loosen cake from rim of pan; cool before removing rim of pan. Melt chocolate pieces and whipping cream over low heat stirring until smooth.
Spread over cheescake. Chill. Garnish with additonal whipping cream, whipped, raspberries and
fresh mint leaves, if desired.

Arizona Sunset Cheesecake

Shortbread Crust

1 1/2 c Flour
1/2 c Finely ground pecans
1/3 c Sugar
1 lg Egg, separated
1/2 c Butter, softened

Cranberry Glaze Filling

1 cn Whole berry cranberry- sauce OR 2 cups cranberry orange relish
2 tb Sugar
1 tb Cornstarch
1 tb Grated lemon zest
1 tb Lemon juice

White Chocolate Filling

1 1/2 c Fresh orange juice
1-3 Inch x 1 inch piece- of orange peel (orange part only)
4 8 oz pkgs cream cheese
2/3 c Sugar
1 tb Grated orange zest
2 tb Cranberry Liqueur (such- as Crantasia Schnapps)
8 oz White chocolate, melted
4 Eggs

Candied Orange Topping

4 c Water
2 c Sugar
3 Seedless oranges (unpeeled)- cut into paper-thin slices

Garnish

Whipped Cream

Shortbread Crust: Preheat the oven to 400 degrees F. Working on a large flat surface, such as a pastry board, place flour, pecans, and sugar in the center of the surface and mix together. Form a small depression or well in the center of the mound. Add the egg yolk and the softened butter to the well, then blend these with the dry mixture. Mix the ingredients thoroughly using your hands -- there is no substitute for warm hands. Shape the dough into a ball and wrap in plastic wrap. Chill for at least 10 minutes. Roll out the dough to a thickness of about 1/4-inch. You should have a circle of about 11 inches in diameter. For best results, roll out your dough between 2 sheets of waxed paper, then peel away the paper and cut the crust in a 9 inch circle. Place the circle inside a 9 inch springform pan. Prick the crust several times with a fork to keep the crust from puffing up during the baking. Place the springform pan in the oven and bake for 15 to 20 minutes, or until light brown. Allow to cool. Using the leftover dough, line the sides of the springform pan. Press the dough against the sides of the pan, smoothing it so as to have a continuous layer of crust all the way around the sides of the pan. Make sure that the side crust meets the bottom crust all the way around. Brush the reserved egg white onto the shell, covering the bottom and sides. This will seal the dough and keep it from becoming soggy. Set aside until ready to use.

Cranberry Glaze Filling:
Mix the sugar and cornstarch together in a small saucepan. Stir in the cranberry sauce. Cook over medium heat, stirring constantly, until thick. Stir in the lemon zest and lemon juice. Set aside to cool slightly.

White Chocolate Filling:
Reset the oven to 350 degrees F. Boil the orange juice and piece of orange peel in a heavy medium saucepan until the juice is reduced to 3 Tbsp - about 12 minutes. Remove and discard the strip of orange peel and set aside the reduced orange juice. Using an electric mixer, beat the cream cheese, sugar, grated orange zest, Crantasia, and reduced orange juice until smooth. Beat in the melted white chocolate and then the eggs, one at a time, beating just until combined. Pour the cranberry glaze filling into the prepared crust, spreading evenly. Pour the white chocolate filling over the cranberry layer and bake about 50 minutes (the top will be dry and the sides puffed slightly - the center will not be set). Move cheesecake to a wire rack and cool completely to room temperature. Chill in the refrigerator overnight.

Candied Oranges Topping:
Cover a wire rack with waxed paper. Set aside. Combine the water and sugar in a heavy shallow wide skillet. Stir over medium heat until the sugar dissolves. Simmer 5 minutes longer. Add the orange slices 1 at a time and adjust the heat so that the syrup bubbles only around the edges of the pan. Cook the oranges for one hour. Turn over the top layer of oranges and cook until the oranges are translucent and the orange peels tender, about another one hour longer. Lift and drain each orange slice out of the syrup, and arrange the slices in a single
layer on the prepared rack. Let dry 1 hour. Boil the orange-sugar syrup until thick, about 6 minutes. Loosen and remove the sides of the springform pan. Set the cheesecake on a serving dish. Overlap the candied orange slices around the top of the cheesecake. Reheat the orange syrup, if necessary, and brush over the orange slices. Drizzle any remainder over each serving. Garnish: whipped cream.
NOTE: You may substitute grapefruits for the oranges in the Candied Oranges Topping if you prefer.

Chocolate Chip Cheesecake Supreme

1 c Chocolate Wafer Crumbs
3 tb Margarine, Melted
24 oz Cream Cheese, Softened
3/4 c Sugar
1/4 c Unbleached All-Purpose Flour
3 ea Large Eggs
1/2 c Sour Cream
1 ts Vanilla
1 c Mini Semi-sweet Chips

Combine crumbs and magarine; press onto bottom of 9-inch springform pan. Bake at 350 degrees F., 10 minutes. Combine cream cheese, sugar and flour, mixing at medium speed on electric mixer until well blended. Add eggs, one at a time, mixing well after each addition. Blend in sour cream and vanilla. Stir in chocolate chips and pour into crust. Bake at 350 degrees F., 55 minutes. Loosen cake from rim of pan; cool before removing rim of pan. Chill. Garnish with whipped cream and fresh mint leaves, if desired.

Cappuccino Cheesecake

1 1/2 c Finely Chopped Nuts
2 tb Sugar
3 tb Margarine, Melted
32 oz Cream Cheese, Softened
1 c Sugar
3 tb Unbleached All-purpose Flour
4 ea Large Eggs
1 c Sour Cream
1 tb Instant Coffee Granules
1/4 ts Cinnamon
1/4 c Boiling water

Combine nuts, sugar, and margarine; press onto bottom of 9-inch spring-form cake pan. Bake at 325 degrees F., 10 minutes. Combine cream cheese, sugar, and flour, mixing at medium speed on electric mixer until well blended. Add eggs, one at a time, mixing well after each addition. Blend in sour cream. Dissolve coffee granules and cinnamon in water. Cool; gradually add to cream cheese mixture, mixing until well blended. Pour over crust. Bake at 450 degrees F., 10 minutes. Reduce oven temperature to 250 degrees F.; continue baking 1 hour. Loosen cake from rim of pan; cool before removing rim of pan. Chill. Garnish with whipped cream and whole coffee beans if desired.

Chocolate Mint Meringue Cheesecake

1 c Chocolate Wafer Crumbs
3 tb Margarine, Melted
2 tb Sugar
24 oz Cream Cheese, Softened
2/3 c Sugar
3 ea Large Eggs
1 c Mint Chocolate Chips, Melted
1 ts Vanilla
3 ea Large Egg Whites
7 oz Marshmallow Creme (1 Jr)

Combine crumbs, margarine and sugar; press onto bottom of 9-inch spring-form pan. Bake at 350 degrees F., 10 minutes. Combine cream cheese and sugar, mixing at medium speed on electric mixer until well blended. Add eggs, one at a time, mixing well after each addition. Blend in mint chocolate and vanilla; pour over crust. Bake at 350 degrees F., 50 minutes. Loosen cake from rim of pan; cool before removing rim of pan. Chill. Beat egg whites until soft peakes form. Gradually add marshmallow creme, beating until stiff peakes form. Carefully spread over top of cheesecake to seal. Bake at 450 degrees F.; 3 to 4 minutes or until lightly browned.

Cherry Cheesecake

1 c Graham Cracker Crumbs
3 tb Sugar
3 tb Margarine, Melted
24 oz Cream Cheese, Softened
3/4 c Sugar
3 ea Large Eggs
1 ts Vanilla
21 oz Cherry Pie Filling (1 cn)

Combine crumbs and margarine; press onto bottom of 9-inch springform pan. Bake at 325 degrees F., 10 minutes. Combine cream cheese and sugar, mixing at medium speed on electric mixer until well blended. Add eggs, one at a time mixing well after each addition. Blend in vanilla; pour over crust. Bake at 450 degrees F., 10 minutes. Reduce oven temperatur to 250 degrees F., continue baking 25 to 30 minutes or until set. Loosen cake from rim of pan; cool before removing rim of pan. Chill. Top with pie filling just before serving.

Chocolate Turtle Cheesecake

2 c Vanilla Wafer Crumbs
6 tb Margarine, Melted
14 oz Carmels (1 bag)
5 oz (1 cn) Evaporated Milk
1 c Chopped Pecans, Toasted
16 oz Cream Cheese, Softened
1/2 c Sugar
1 ts Vanilla
2 ea Large Eggs
1/2 c Semi-sweet Chocolate Chips *
* Chocolate chips should be melted.

Combine crumbs and margarine, press onto bottom and sides of 9-inch spring- form pan. Bake at 350 degrees F., 10 minutes. In 1 1/2-quart heavy saucepan, melt carmels with milk over low heat, stirring frequently, until smooth. Pour over crust. Top with pecans. Combine cream cheese, sugar and vanila, mixing at medium speed on electric mixer until well blended. Add eggs, one at a time, mixing well after each addition. Blend in chocolate, pour over pecans. Bake at 350 degrees F., 40 minutes. Loosen cake from rim of pan; cool before removing rim of pan. Chill. Garnish with
whipped cream, additional chopped nuts and maraschino cherries, if desired.

Chocolate Orange Supreme Cheesecake

1 c Chocolate Wafer Crumbs
1/4 ts Cinnamon
3 tb Margarine, Melted
32 oz Cream Cheese, Softened
3/4 c Sugar
4 ea Large Eggs
1/2 c Sour Cream
1 ts Vanilla
1/2 c Semi-sweet Choc. ChipsMelted
2 tb Orange Flavored Liqueur
1/2 ts Grated Orange Peel

Combine crumbs, cinnamon and margarine; press onto bottom of 9-inch spring- form pan. Bake at 325 degrees F., 10 minutes. Combine cream cheese and sugar, mixing at medium speed on electric mixer until well blended. Add eggs, one at a time, mixing well after each addition. Blend in sour cream and vanilla. Blend chocolate into 3 cups batter; blend liqueur and pell into remaining batter. Pour chocolate batter over crust. Bate at 350 degrees F., 30 minutes. Reduce oven temperature to
325 degrees F. Spoon remianing batter over chocolate batter continue baking 30 minutes more. Loosen cake from rim of pan; cool before removing rim of pan. Chill.

Cocoa-Nut Meringue Cheesecake

7 oz (1 pk) Flaked Coconut *
1/4 c Chopped pecans
3 tb Margarine, Melted
16 oz Cream Cheese, Softened
1/3 c Sugar
3 tb Cocoa
2 tb Water
1 ts Vanilla
3 ea Large Eggs, Separated
Dash salt
7 oz (1 jr) Marshmallow Creme
1/2 c Chopped Pecans
* Coconut should be flaked and toasted.

Combine coconut, pecans, and margarine, press onto bottom of 9-inch springform pan. Combine cream cheese, sugar, cocoa, water and vanilla, mixing at medium speed on electric mixer until well blended. Blend in egg yolks, pour over crust. Bake at 350 degrees F., 30 minutes. Loosen cake from rim of pan, cool before removing rim of pan. Beat egg whites and salt until foamy, gradually add marshmallow creme, beating until stiff peaks form. Sprinkle pecans over cheesecake to within 1/2-inch of outer edge. Carefully spread marshmallow creme mixture over top of cheescake to
seal. Bake at 350 degrees F., 15 minutes. Cool.

Tempting Trifle Cheesecake

1 1/2 c Soft Coconut Macaroons*
3/4 c Sugar
1/2 c Whipping cream
2 tb Sweet Sherry
10 oz Red Raspberry Preserves
1 x Toasted Slivered Almonds
24 oz Cream Cheese, Softened
4 ea Large Eggs
1/2 c Sour Cream
1 ts Vanilla
1/2 c Whipping Cream, Whipped
* Soft coconut macroon cookies crumbs.

Press crumbs onto bottom of greased 9-inch springform pan. Bake at 325 degrees F., 15 minutes. Combine cream cheese and sugar, mixing at medium speed on electric mixture until well blended. Add eggs, one at a time, mixing well after each addition. Blend in sour cream, whipping cream, sherry and vanilla; pour over crust. Bake at 325 degrees F., 1 hour and 10 minutes. Loosen cake from rim of pan; cool befroe removing rim of pan. Chill. Heat preserves in saucepan over low heat until melted. Strain to remove seeds. Spoon over cheesecake, spreading to edges. Dollop with
whipped cream; top with almonds.

Chapter 4:

Recipes from South of the Border

GRILLED CHICKEN QUESADILLAS

1 Whole chicken breast -- boneless & skinless
2 tablespoons   Vegetable oil
1/4 teaspoon   Salt
Chili powder (4 pinches)
1/4 teaspoon   Cumin
1/4 teaspoon   Black pepper
1 Clove of Garlic -- minced
1 Problano Chili
8 6-inch   Flour Tortillas
2 cups   Grated cheddar cheese (mild -- or sharp)
1 cup   Grated chihuahua cheese or -- Montery Jack cheese
1 cup   Salsa or guacamole -optional

[Note: the serving size (24) is the number of pieces you will get -- not necessarily how many people it will feed.]

1. Heat grill or broiler and cook chicken until done (approx. 5 minutes on each side). Cool to room temperature and shred into 1/4-inch pieces.

2. Over gas burner or under broiler, place poblano pepper and char skin until black all over, rotate as necessary. Place pepper in a bag and close. After about 15 minutes remove pepper from bag and remove charred skin, seeds, and stem. Cut pepper into 1/2-inch strips.

3. Place 4 tortillas on table and top each with 3/4 cup of cheese, a pinch of chili powder, 1/2 cup of shredded chicken and divided poblano strips. Top with remaining tortillas.

4. Heat an 8-inch or larger skillet -- dry, no oil -- over medium high heat. Place quesadilla, one at a time in skillet and cook until golden brown (about 1 minute) Turn over and cook another minute.

5. Let cool slightly before cutting into 6 wedges. Serve with salsa or guacamole if desired.

Homemade Taco Sauce

12 each   Canning tomatoes
1 cup   Chopped green chili
1 teaspoon   Cumino
1 each   Sm onion
1 teaspoon   Salt
1 teaspoon   Oregano

Dip tomatoes in boiling water, peel and chop. Chop small onions. Put tomato, onion and chili in 6 quart pan. Add seasonings and simmer for 1 1/2 hours. Put in canning jars. Bath in hot water bath for 30 min.

HOT & SPICY CHICKEN QUESADILLAS

2 teaspoons   Olive oil
2 Boneless chicken breasts -- cut into strips
2 tablespoons   Chili sauce
1 Jalapeno pepper -- seeded and
4 Eight inch flour tortillas
1 cup   Shredded Cheddar cheese
4 teaspoons   Canola oil or plain -- vegetable oil

Preheat the Calphalon Solo Griddle on medium heat on top of the stove. Add the olive oil to the hot pan. Place the chicken strips, chili sauce and jalapeno pepper in the pan and saute until cooked through, approx. 3-5 minutes. Remove and reserve.

Wipe the pan clean.

Place the chicken mixture on one half of each of the 4 flour tortillas.
Sprinkle with cheese and fold over to form a half circle.

Again, preheat the Calphalon Solo Griddle on medium. Oil the cooking
surface with one tsp. Canola oil. Place a filled tortilla on the cooking surface. Cook until light brown. Turn. Repeat with the other three tortillas. Slice each tortilla into three wedges and serve with salsa and black beans.

Serves 4

Hot Chile Sauce

2 cups	Water
	Chilies -- *
1/4 cup	Red Wine Vinegar
1 teaspoon	Dry Mustard
1 each	Clove Garlic
1/4 cup	Olive Oil

* You should use 6 to 8 dried Cascabel chilies in this recipe. If they can't be found, then use a 1/2 of a medium Ancho Chile. But the result will not be as hot.
Heat water to boiling; stir in chilies. Boil uncovered 5
minutes; drain. Remove stems. Place chilies, vinegar, mustard and garlic in a blender container; cover and blend until the chilies are finely chopped. Gradually pour in oil, blending until smooth. Makes about 1/2 cup of sauce.

Hot Pickled Vegetables

4 ounces	Green Beans -- Whole
3 each	Celery; Stalks -- *
1 cup	Carrots; 2 med -- **
1 1/2 cups	Cauliflowerets
1 cup	Broccoli Flowerets
1 cup	Pearl Onions
1/2 cup	Peppers -- ***
1/2 cup	Coarse Salt
2 cups	Cider Vinegar
2 cups	Water
2 tablespoons	Black Peppercorns
1/4 teaspoon	Cloves -- Ground

* Celery should be cut into 2 X 1/4-inch strips (about 1 1/2 Cups) ** Carrots should be cut diagonally into thin slices. *** Peppers can be canned or fresh. Use Serrano or Jalapeno Chiles
Mix all ingredients in a large glass or plastic container. Cover and refrigerate at least 48 hours but no longer than 2 weeks. Makes about 10 cups of vegetable relish.

Huevos Rancheros

3 tablespoons	butter
2 tablespoons	onion -- finely chopped
1 clove	garlic -- minced
2 tablespoons	green pepper -- finely chopped
6 eggs	
1 tablespoon	picante sauce
2 tablespoons	mild salsa

Melt butter in large frying pan. Saute onions, garlic, and pepper until soft. Beat eggs until light and pour into frying pan. Cook over very low heat, stirring constantly. When eggs begin to harden, add picante sauce and salsa, continuing to cook and stir until eggs are set. Serve immediately.

Serving Ideas : Serve with flour tortillas, grated cheese, and salsa.

NOTES : A great, easy brunch dish, especially with Grapefruit-Avocado Salad, and Tequila Sunrises.

JALAPENO CHICKEN FAJITAS

8	ounces	Boneless chicken breasts
1/4	cup	Lime juice
2	tablespoons	Water
1		Clove garlic

Jalapeno Flavor Process -- Cheese Product
Lettuce
Green onions
Tomatoes
Ripe olives
Flour tortillas

Marinate chicken breasts in lime juice, water and garlic. Broil or grill chicken; slice thinly and serve in flour tortillas with other ingredients.

Makes 8 fajitas.

Jalapeno Cream Sauce

1	each	Jalapeno Peppers -- *
1	each	Clove Garlic -- Finely Chopped
2	teaspoons	Vegetable Oil
1/8	teaspoon	Salt

Pepper -- Dash Of

-----QUICK CREME FRAICHE-----
1/3 cup   Whipping Cream
2/3 cup   Dairy Sour Cream

* Jalapeno peppers shoud be seeded and finely chopped. You should use no more than 2 depending on how hot you want it.
Cook chile(s) and garlic in oil over low heat, stirring
frequently, until tender, about 4 minutes. Remove from heat; stir in
remaining ingredients including the creme fraiche. Makes about 1 1/4 cups of sauce. QUICK CREME FRAICHE: Gradually stir whipping cream into sour cream. Cover and refrigerate up to 48 hours.

SUPPER NACHOS

1 pound	Ground beef
1/2 cup	Onion -- chopped
1 teaspoon	Seasoned salt -- optional
1/2 teaspoon	Cumin
2 cans	Refried beans
1 package	Taco seasoning mix
2 cups	Monterey Jack Cheese -- grated
¼ cup	Green chiles -- diced
1 cup	Cheddar cheese -- grated
2/3 cup	Salsa
	Tortilla chips
1 cup	Guacamole seasoning -- optional
½ cup	Sour cream -- optional
¼ cup	Chopped green onions -- optional
1 cup	Sliced olives -- optional

1. Heat skillet at med-hi temperature; brown meat and onions.
2. Drain well in colander removing all grease.
3. Return meat and onions to skillet add cumin and mix well.
4. In a large mixing bowl, combine refried beans and taco seasoning mix; blend well.
5. Add grated M. Jack cheese to bean mixture; mix together.
6. Spread refried beans in shallow rectangular 9 x 13 pan.
7. cover bean mixture with browned meat and onions.
8. Sprinkle chiles evenly over meat. Top with grated chedder cheese. 9. Pour salsa over cheese.(May be made ahead and refrigerated at this point~DO NOT FREEZE!)
10. Bake uncovered in 400 degrees oven for 20 to 25 minutes or until thoroughly heated.
11. Place tortilla chips around edge of meat/beans dish and garnish as desired.

LA FOGATA'S GREEN CHICKEN ENCHILADAS

¼ pound	Tomatillos -- quartered
½ cup	Water
1	Clove garlic -- whole
2	Serrano chiles
¼ teaspoon	Salt
¼ teaspoon	Pepper
1/3 cup	Cilantro leaves -- loosely
Chicken stock -- if needed	
2	Whole chicken breasts
	Lightly salted water
1 cup	Chicken stock
1 cup	Peanut oil
8	Corn tortillas
1 cup	Sour cream
1 pound	Mozzarella cheese -- grated

Boil tomatillos in water with garlic,chiles,salt and pepper until soft,about 15-20 minutes. puree cooked sauce in blender to liquefy. While blending,add washed cilantro leaves. Set aside. the sauce yield is about 2and1/2 cups. It will thicken upon standing and you may need to thin with chicken stock. simmer chicken in lightly salted water until tender about 10-15 minutes. Cool chicken will be slightly undercooked. Shred cooked chicken and then,just prior to serving,heat in 1 cup chicken stock. This will heat chicken without overcooking. In medium skillet,heat oil to 300 degrees. Pass tortillas into hot oil for a few seconds to soften and seal. Remove carefully and set aside between paper towels. Do this just prior to assembly fill softened tortillas with shredded chicken and 1-2 tablespoons sauce. Roll up and place seam-side-down in casserole. Pour green sauce over top and garnish with sour cream and cheese. place in 375-degree oven 5-8 minutes or just long enough to melt cheese.

Note:Sauce may be made a day in advance,but the dish is best when chicken is freshly prepared.

LAZY ENCHILADAS

1 medium	Onion chopped
1/2 medium	Red/green pepper chopped
2	Cloves garlic minced
9	10 med mushrooms sliced -- thinly
1	15oz can stewed tomatoes -- with juice
½ cup	Frozen corn kernels
1	15-oz can black beans -- rinsed
½ teaspoon	Cinnamon
½ -1 tsp.	oregano
1 tablespoon	Chili powder(maybe more)
1 2tsp	cumin (maybe more start -- with one)
or	more of cayenne
4	Flour tortillas (not the huge -- size, more if you do)

1. Water saute onion,pepper garlic, until onion translucent.
2. Add spices and let them coat the onion mixture.
3. Add mushrooms and let cook briefly for 1-2 minutes.
4. Add can of stewed tomatoes and bring to simmer.
5. Reduce heat and simmer for 10 minutes.
6. Add corn and simmer for 10 more minutes.
7. Add beans and simmer for 5 minutes.
8. Warm tortillas so they are pliable, and with a slotted spoon scoop mixture in tortilla, roll, and place on dinner plate. With tablespoon, take liquid and pour over tortillas. Repeat until done.

Serves 2 -3 people, depending on side dishes and hunger:)
NOTE: Simmering times are approximate, but you essentially want to let it cook so the flavors have combined, but not to reduce to a true stew. It should look a soupy stew, so that you have liquid to put on tortillas.

Lentils with Chilies, Pork, and Fruit

1/2 pound	(1 heaped cup) lentils -- brown if available
1/2 small	White onion
	Sea salt to taste
	The pork:
1 pound	Boneless stewing pork -- cut
	1-inch cubes
	Sea salt to taste
	The seasoning and final -- cooking:
5 small	Chilies anchos -- cleaned of
	and seeds and
	Lightly toasted
¼ pound	Tomatoes -- broiled
1	Garlic clove -- peeled and
	chopped
¼ teaspoon	Dried oregano -- Mexican if
1	Whole clove
1 1/2	Inch cinnamon stick
1 tablespoon	Melted lard or safflower oil
1 medium	Plantain (about 8-oz) -- peeled and cut into
	¼ Inch cubes
2	Thick pineapple slices -- peeled, cored, and c
	Small triangular wedges

The lentils: Run the lentils through your hands to make sure there are no stones or other foreign bodies in them. Rinse them in two changes of water and put into a pan. Add onion, salt to taste, and enough water to come about 2 inches above the surface of the lentils. Set over medium heat and bring to a fast simmer. Continue simmering until the lentils are quite soft ~ about 3 hours, depending on their age. Keep a pan of near-boiling water on the side, ready to add if necessary.

Put the pork pieces into a pan; add salt to taste and water to cover.
Bring to a fast simmer and continue simmering until the pork is tender but not soft - about 25 minutes. Strain, reserving the broth, and set broth and meat aside.

Cover the dried chilies with boiling water and leave to soak for about 15 minutes, until the chilies have softened and become fleshy. Drain and put into a blender with 1 cup of the reserved pork broth, the broiled tomatoes, garlic, oregano, clove, and cinnamon; blend until smooth, adding more broth only if needed to release the blades of the blender.

Heat the lard in a small frying pan, add the blended ingredients, and fry over medium heat, stirring and scraping the bottom of the pan, until reduced and well seasoned - about 4 minutes. Add to the lentils and add the pork, remaining broth, plantain, and pineapple; simmer together for about 30 minutes. Adjust salt and add water if necessary. The mixture should be like a thick soup.

Lime Butter Sauce

2 each   Egg Yolks -- Large
1 tablespoon   Lime Juice
½ cup   Butter -- NOT Margarine
½ teaspoon   Lime Peel -- Grated

Stir egg yolks and lime juice vigorously in a 1 1/2-quart saucepan.
Add 1/4 cup of the butter. Heat over very low heat, stirring constantly, until butter is melted. Add remaining butter. Continue heating, stirring vigorously, until butter is melted and sauce is thickening. (Be sure butter melts slowly so that sauce will thicken without curdling.) Stir in lime peel. Serve hot or at room temperature. Cover and refrigerate any remaining sauce. Makes about 3/4 cup of Lime Hollandaise sauce.

Chapter 5:

120 Lip-Smacking Good Jam Recipes

Fresh Strawberry Jam

6 cup strawberries -- sliced
2 boxes pectin
1 3/4 cup honey
2 tablespoon lemon juice

In saucepan, combine strawberries and pectin, mashing or crushing berries to blend completely. Bring mixture to a boil. Boil hard for one minute, stirring constantly. Add honey and lemon juice. Return to a rolling boil for five minutes, stirring constantly. Remove from heat. Skim off foam. Ladle into hot sterilized jars. Seal. Makes eight 1/2 pints.

Ginger Peach Jam

4 1/2 cup prepared fruit (about 3 1/4 lbs full; ly ripe peaches)
1/4 cup finely chopped crystallized ginger
6 cup sugar
1 box sure-jell fruit pectin

Peel and pit peaches; finely chop or grind. Measure 4 1/2 cups into 6- to 8-quart saucepot; add ginger.

Measure sugar and set aside. Mix fruit pectin into fruit in saucepot. Place over high heat and stir until mixture comes to a full boil. Immediately add all sugar and stir. B ring to a full rolling boil and boil 1 minute, stirring constantly. Remove from heat and skim off foam with metal spoon. Ladle quickly into hot jars, filling within 1/8 inch of tops. Wipe jar rims and threads. Cover with two-piece lids. Screw bands tightly. Invert jars for 5 minutes, then turn upright. After 1 hour, check seals.*

*Or follow water bath method recommended by USDA.

Makes about 8 (1 cup) jars

Gooseberry Jam

1 lb gooseberries
3/4 lb sugar

Stem gooseberries and wash carefully. Drain. Add sugar. Heat very slowly in a covered container until juice begins to form. Uncover and boil until juice sheets from spoon.

Grandma Howard's Tomato Jam

1/2 orange
1/2 lemon
3 cup tomatoes; peeled, chopped about 1 3
1 pkg pectin crystals; 57 g
4 1/2 cup sugar, granulated

Halve and seed orange and lemon. In food processor, finely shop fruit with rind. Transfer to heavy saucepan; add tomatoes and bring to a boil. Reduce heat and simmer for 10 minutes or until rind is tender. Stir in pectin. Return to boil; boil for 1 minute, stirring. Stir in sugar; bring to a full rolling boil. Boil, stirring, for 1 minute. Remove from heat and skim off foam. Pour into hot sterilized jars, leaving 1/4 inch head space. Seal jars; process in boiling water bath for 10 minutes. Store in cool, dark, dry place. MAKES: ABOUT 5 CUPS

Ground Cherry Jam

2 lb ground cherries; 8 c husked
4 cup sugar
1 cup water
2 lemons; grated rind & juice

Husk and wash the ground cherries carefully. Measure the sugar and water into a large kettle. Bring to a full rolling boil, and boil for 2 minutes.

Add the cherries, lemon rinds, and juice. Bring to a full rolling boil again, reduce heat and simmer for 5 minutes. Remove from heat, cover with a clean towel, and let stand overnight.

Next day, return to the heat, and again bring to boil. Reduce heat and cook gently until transparent (about 15 minutes). Immediately pour into hot, sterilized glasses seal at once.

Yields 5 to 6 cups.

Instant Raspberry Cordial Jam

12 oz raspberry jam
1 tablespoon to 2 chambord or other
1 raspberry liqueur

Stir liqueur into jam; cover and refrigerate at least one day to allow flavors to meld.

Island Jam

4 cup cantaloupe, peeled and
1 diced
3 oranges, peeled and diced
1/4 cup lemon juice
4 cup sugar
1 teaspoon lemon rind
1 teaspoon orange rind
1/2 teaspoon salt
3 cup bananas

Combine cantaloupe, oranges, and 1/4 cup lemon juice in heavy saucepan. Bring to a boil and simmer for 15 minutes. Add sugar, lemon rind, orange rind, and salt. Continue simmering for 30 minutes. Add 3 cups sliced bananas and continue simmering for an additional 15 minutes. Pour into jelly jars and cover with paraffin. Can be frozen. Yield 8 (6 ounce) jars.

Pear & Ginger Jam

2 lb pears
4 oz (1/2 cup) preserved ginger
2 lb (5 1/3 cups) sugar
1 1/4 cup water
1 oz (1) fresh ginger
1 juice of 2 lemons

Makes 2 lbs Peel, core and dice the pears. Cut the preserved ginger into small chunks. Put all the ingredients into a preserving kettle and stir over a gentle heat until the sugar has dissolved. Bring to a boil and boil rapidly for about t 10 minutes, stirring occasionally, or until setting point is reached. Remove the piece of fresh ginger, lift out the fruit with a slotted spoon and place in hot clean jars. Rapidly boil the syrup to reduce for a few minute s, then pour over the fruit to cover. Cover and process, then complete seals and cool.

Pear-Apple Jam

2 cup finely chopped pears (peeled & core; d)
1 cup finely chopped apples (peeled & cor; ed)
6 1/2 cup sugar
1/4 teaspoon ground cinnamon
1/3 cup bottled lemon juice
6 oz liquid pectin

Yield: About 7 to 8 half-pints

Procedure: Crush apples and pears in a large saucepan and stir in cinnamon. Thoroughly mix sugar and lemon juice with fruits and bring to a boil over high heat, stirring constantly. Immediately stir in pectin. Bring to a full rolling boil and boil hard 1 minute, stirring constantly. Remove from heat, quickly skim off foam, and fill sterile jars leaving 1/4-inch head space.

Adjust lids and process as recommended in Table 1.

Table 1. Recommended process time for Pear-Apple Jam in a boiling water canner.

Style of Pack: Hot. Jar Size: Half-Pints. Process Time at Altitudes
of 0 - 1,000 ft: 5 min.
1,001 - 6,000 ft: 10 min.
Above 6,000 ft: 15 min.

Pineapple-Apricot Jam

20 oz pineapple; crushed, 1 cn
6 oz maraschino cherries; 1 jar,*
8 oz dried apricots; cut into 1/4
1/4 cup water
3 1/2 cup sugar
2 tablespoon lemon juice
3 oz fruit pectin; liquid,1 pouch

*   Drain, reserving 1/3 cup of the syrup, the cherries and cut up in small pieces.

Heat the pineapple, with the syrup, the reserved cherry syrup, the apricots and the water to boiling in a Dutch oven, stirring occasionally then reduce the heat and cover. Simmer, stirring occasionally, until the apricots are tender, about 10 minutes. Stir in the sugar, lemon juice, and cherries. Heat to a full rolling boil over high heat, stirring constantly. Boil and stir for 1 minute. Remove from the heat and stir in the pectin. Pour into hot sterilized jars or glasses or freezer containers. Cover and cool to room temperature and store in the refrigerator or freezer no more than 3 months.

Quick Spiced Peach Jam

2 tablespoon water
2 tablespoon lemon juice
1/4 teaspoon cloves
1/2 teaspoon cinnamon
4 cup cut-up peaches
3 cup sugar

Combine the water, lemon juice, cloves and cinnamon in a quart saucepan.
Dip the peaches in boiling water for 30 seconds and rinse in cold water. Peel and cut in small pieces into a measuring cup. Add them a cup full at a time to the saucepan, giving them a quick stir. When all the peaches are in the saucepan, bring to a boil and cook until soft, stirring frequently. This should take 6-8 minutes.
Stirring with one hand, add the sugar with the other. Stir over moderate heat until he mixture boils. Increase the heat and cook until the mixture thickens or measure 220 degrees F on the thermometer.
Pour into hot, clean jars, leaving 1/4 inch head space. Wipe the rims and put on the lids and screw bands very firmly, then process in a boiling water bath for 10 minutes. Cool, label and store in a dark place.

Rose Hip Jam

4 quart rose hips with black ends
1   removed
1   (about 5 pounds)
3 1/2 cup sugar
1 x water (wine or sherry)

Gather the rose hips after the first frost. I am not sure why this is done but I have several sources that say to do it, including my grandmother, so I wait. Wash the rose hips well in case there is any insecticide residue. Cover with water and simmer until the hips are very soft and falling apart. Press through a food mill or colander to remove the seeds and larger particles. Press through a finer sieve to remove the smaller fibers and seed bits.

Cook the pulp down until it is quite thick. How thick? That is hard to say. Thicker than heavy cream. I check the measurements at this point. I add about a pound of sugar for every pound of pulp. The 3 1/2 cups is my measurement from the last time I made this.

Add the sugar and check the taste. Sometimes I add a bit more sugar. Rose hips have enough pectin to jell and enough ascorbic acid to make it a little tart. Cook over high heat until the mixture has a thick jam-like consistency. Put in jars. Makes 4 half-pint jars

Rose Petal Jam

30 large red cabbage roses
3 lb sugar
2 pint water
1/2 lemon

Take the roses and cut off the white ends. Make a syrup with the sugar and water. Then add the juice of the half a lemon and the rose petals. Boil until the roses crystallize, stirring frequently with a wooden spoon. Turkish cooks keep this for years.

Sherried Pear & Cranberry Jam

1 1/2 cup fresh or frozen cranberries,
1   about 1/2lb (250g)
4   (or 5) ripe pears, about 2lb
5 cup granulated sugar
1/2 cup water
1/4 cup sherry
1   box certo crystals fruit
1   pectin

Place cranberries in a food processor and whirl, using an on-and-off motion, until coarsely ground. Turn into a large bowl. Peel, core and finely chop pears. They should measure about 2 cups. (Do not chop in food processor; they will turn to mush.) Add chopped pears to cranberries. Stir in sugar until well mixed. Let stand for 10 minutes. Then, combine water, sherry and fruit pectin crystals in a small saucepan. Bring to a boil and boil for 1 minute, stirring constantly. Stir into fruit mixture. Continue stirring for 3 minutes. (There will be a few sugar crystals remaining.) Immediately pour into jars. Cover at once with tight lids. Let stand at room temperature until set. It may take up to 24 hours. Then, store in the refrigerator or freezer. Jam will keep well in the refrigerator for up to 3 weeks or in the freezer for several months. Makes 6 1/2 cups.

Apricot, Orange & Almond Jam

1 lb dried apricots
2 oz split almonds
3 oranges
2 lemons
2 1/2 lb sugar
2 1/2 teaspoon ground cinnamon

Chop the apricots roughly. Put them into a large bowl, sprinkling the fine grated zest of the oranges and the cinnamon between layers. Squeeze the
juice of the oranges, measure and add enough water to make 3 pints in all. Pour the liquids over the fruit and leave to soak overnight in a cool place.

Slide the contents of the bowl into a preserving pan and simmer gently until the fruit is beautifully tender. Check the fruit occasionally
as it cooks and crush it down into the pan with a potato masher. It may need   1-1/4 hours to become really soft.

Warm the sugar. Add it to the pan together with the juice of the lemons and the almonds. Cook gently until the sugar is melted, then fast-boil   until the saucer test shows that the preserve will set. Pot, tie down and label the preserve in the usual way. Makes enough to fill 5 jars.

Chapter 6:

The Ultimate Chicken Wing cookbook

Barbecued Chicken Wings

35	Chicken wings -- tips removed
1	Stick butter
1 cup	Brown sugar
½ tablespoon	Sauce
½ cup	Dry red wine
2 teaspoons	Dry mustard
2 large	Garlic cloves -- crushed
¼ cup	Fresh lemon juice
	Fresh ground pepper to taste

Requires marinating and long cooking time but it is simple. Place chicken wings, disjointed, in large flat pan. Combine other ingredients and pour over chicken.
Let stand for at least 1 hour or overnight. Be sure all wings are well coated with marinade. Place pan in 350 oven and reduce heat to 250. Bake 4-5 hours, turning wings at regular intervals. If all marinade is not absorbed, pour off and dry wings out a bit longer in oven (but not too much) before serving.

Beau's Sweet-Sour Chicken Wings

20	Chicken wings
7 ½ ounces	Tomato sauce (half can)
2 tablespoons	Orange marmalade
1 tablespoon	Honey
2 teaspoons	Ginger -- minced
2 teaspoons	Fermented chili sauce -- (Summit brand)
2 teaspoons	Pepper vinegar
4	Garlic cloves -- peeled
1 teaspoon	Salt (scant)
2 teaspoons	MSG
½ cup	Water (more as needed)

ds Tabasco, to taste -(or other hot pepper
 -sauce)

Cut off spurs from chicken wing-tips and rinse chicken wings. Place in pressure cooker with water; bring to pressure and cook at high heat for up to five minutes. Remove from pressure cooker and place cooked-out fat in wide-mouthed, tapered jar for other uses.

Blend all ingredients except chicken and Tabasco (or hot sauce) until fairly even consistency, with no large chunks of ginger or garlic.

Place 3/4 of sauce in pan. Roll wings in sauce; remove wings to broiler pan (with slotted top). Bake at 325 degrees F. for 20 minutes. Remove from oven and spoon about half of remaining sauce on top of each piece; broil for 5 minutes. Add Tabasco or other hot pepper sauces to taste and serve.

Beau's notes:

* Use vinegar "which has been used to keep a supply of bird's-eye peppers."
* After discarding chicken spurs, wash hands with very warm water and Dial soap (and follow up with isopropyl alcohol rinse); wash all utensils with bleach. (One should always regard chickens, even if processed in USA or inspected by USDA, as unclean! USDA inspectors are notoriously less than thorough, and U.S. packing houses often neglect basic hygienic rules in working with chickens, especially in dealing with their entrails, waste products un-excreted, etc. And one should not expect much better from out-of-country chickens.)

-

BEAUJOLAIS-GLAZED CHICKEN WINGS

3 pounds	Chicken wings -- tips removed at joints into 2 pcs
1/3 cup	Soy sauce
1/3 cup	Orange juice
2/3 cup	Dry red wine
2 tablespoons	Dry red wine -- (additional)
3	Cloves garlic -- mashed
2 tablespoons	Ginger root -- chopped
6 tablespoons	Red currant jelly
2 tablespoons	Orange zest -- grated
1 tablespoon	Orange zest -- thin julienne For garnish

1. Place split wings in a large shallow nonaluminum pan. Mix soy, orange juice, red wine, garlic and ginerrroot together and pour over the wings. Cover pan with plastic wrap and refrigerate overnight, turning several times in the marinade. 2. 375. Line a baking pan with foil. Coat a cooking cooking spray and place rack in baking pan. 3. Drain chicken and arrange on once. Remove from oven, but do not turn off the oven.
4. Combine jelly, 2 T Stir until jelly is melted.
Brush wings generously with the glaze and return to oven for 10 minutes. Turn and brush again with glaze.
Bake another 10 minutes, or until a rich dark brown and shiny. Remove and cool minutes. Can be baked up to a day ahead and reheated. 5. Arrange in overlap

Betty White's Chicken Wings Pacifica

3 pounds	chicken wings
½ cup	butter or margarine
1 cup	soy sauce
1 cup	brown sugar
¾ cup	water
½ teaspoon	dry mustard

Arrange wings in shallow baking pan. Heat butter, soy sauce, sugar, water and mustard until butter and sugar melt. Cool; pour over wings and marinate at least 2 hours, turning once or twice. Bake in same pan at 375: for 1-1/4 to 1-1/2 hours, turning occasionally. Drain on paper towels.

Blue Cheese Dip

2 ounces	Blue cheese -- crumbled
½ cup	Sour cream
½ cup	Mayonnaise

Place everything in food processor and process till smooth.
Chill.   Serve with celery sticks and Buffalo Chicken Wings

BLUE CORNMEAL CHICK WINGS

¼ cup	Lime juice
¼ cup	Oil
½ teaspoon	Crushed red pepper
10	Chicken wings -- about 2 lb
2 tablespoons	Margarine or butter
½ cup	Blue or yellow cornmeal
2 tablespoons	Flour
½ teaspoon	Salt
½ teaspoon	Ground cumin
1/8 teaspoon	Pepper

Mix lime juice, oil and red pepper in large glass or plastic bowl. Cut eac chicken wing at joints to make 3 pieces. Discard tip. Cut off and discard excess skin.
Place wings in oil mixture and stir to coat. Cover and refrig 3 hours, stirring occasionally. Drain. Heat oven to 425F. Heat margarine Shake remaining ingredients in plastic bag or mix in bowl. Shake wings in cornmeal mixture to coat and place in pan. Bake, uncovered, 20 minutes. Turn. Bake until golden brown, 20 to 25 minutes longer.

Broiled Chicken Wings

1 pound	chicken wings
3 tablespoons	lemon juice
3 tablespoons	soy sauce
1/8 teaspoon	onion powder
	salt -- to taste
	pepper -- to taste
1 tablespoon	honey
1 tablespoon	catsup

Remove tips from wings; cut wings into 2 pieces, and place in a shallow dish. Combine lemon juice, soy sauce, and onion powder; pour over chicken. Cover and marinate wings in refrigerator several hours or overnight. Drain chicken wings, reserving 1 tablespoon marinade; place wings on a foil-lined broiler pan. Sprinkle with salt and pepper. Combine reserved marinade, honey, and catsup, stirring well; brush half of mixture on chicken wings. Broil 6 to 7 inches from broiler for 7 minutes. Turn and brush with remaining sauce; broil 7 additional minutes.

BRONZED CHICKEN WINGS WITH YOUNG GINGER

2 pounds	Chicken wings
¼ cup	Dark corn syrup
¼ cup	Soy sauce
1 tablespoon	Corn oil
2 teaspoons	Minced fresh ginger
2 tablespoons	Dry sherry
¼ pound	Very small mushrooms
1/2	Sliced bamboo shoots
2	Green onions -- cut in 2"
½ cup	Chicken broth
1 tablespoon	Cornstarch
2 tablespoons	Water

Cut wing tips off chicken wings. Place in shallow baking dish. In small bowl, stir together corn syrup and soy sauce. Pour over chicken wings; toss to coat well. Marinate 30 minutes. Drain; reserve marinade.

In large heavy skillet, heat corn oil over medium heat. Add chicken wings and ginger; stir fry 2 minutes. Stir in reserved marinade and sherry. Add mushrooms, bamboo shoots and green onions; stirring frequently, cook 2 minutes. Add chicken broth. Bring to boil. Reduce heat; cover and simmer 20 minutes or until tender. Remove chicken wings to serving platter, keep warm.

Stir together cornstarch and water until smooth. Stir into skillet. Stirring constantly, bring to boil over medium heat and boil 1 minute. Spoon over chicken wings. Makes 4 servings.

Buffalo Chicken Wings

3 pounds	Chicken wings -- Salt and pepper
1	Bottle Crystal's sauce

-----FOR DIP-----

1 ounce	Crumbled bleu cheese
1/3 cup	Mayonnaise
2 tablespoons	Milk
	Celery sticks

Lop the tips off the chicken wings and cut into drummettes. Discard tips or use for stock. Bake drummettes in a flat pan at 350 degrees for 25 minutes. Drain pan juices into stock pot for future use. Add Crystal's Sauce, either medium or hot, and cook another 20 minutes. Prepare dip by mixing and arrange all on a platter while piping hot. The wings are traditionally served with bleu cheese and celery.

BUFFALO CHICKEN WINGS #2

2 pounds	Chicken Wings
	Oil For Frying
½ cup	Butter
1 tablespoon	Tabasco Sauce
1 tablespoon	Hot Pepper Sauce
	Blue Cheese Dressing
	Chilled Celery Sticks

Fry up the chicken wings that have had the tips removed and cut in half at the joint in 1/4 cup of butter until golden brown. Allow the wings to cool before frying a second time, yes they are fried a second time so if you are a calorie watcher you can stop now. They can be fried the first time a day ahead. Before frying the second time mix the Tabasco and Hot Pepper sauce with the melted butter. Fry the wings a second time in the HOT butter until wings are heated. You need to use enough Tabasco and Hot Pepper sauce to give the butter a reddish color. Serve with chilled celery sticks and blue cheese dressing.

BUFFALO CHICKEN WINGS #3

2 pounds	Chicken Wings
	Salad Oil
1 tablespoon	Tabasco Sauce
¼ cup	Melted Butter
	Celery Sticks
	Carrot Sticks
	Blue Cheese Dressing

Cut tips off wings and cut wing in half at the joint. In a 4 quart saucepan, heat 2 inches of salad oil to 375oF. Lower wings into oil. Fry chicken wings for 15 minutes or until very tender. Drain on paper towel. Meanwhile, in a large bowl, stir together Tabasco Sauce and butter until well blended. Add the chicken wings and toss gently to coat well. Serve with blue cheese dressing, chilled celery sticks and chilled carrot sticks.

BUFFALO CHICKEN WINGS #4

½ cup	Miracle Whip
¼ cup	Sour Cream
¼ pound	Blue Cheese
4	Ribs Celery
1	Small Onion
2	Cloves Garlic
1 tablespoon	Oil
½	Lemon
8 ounces	Tomato Sauce
¼ cup	Tabasco Sauce
½ teaspoon	Salt
3 pounds	Chicken Wings
	Oil For Frying

Combine Miracle Whip and sour cream. Crumble and stir in the blue cheese. Cut the celery into sticks. Chop onion and mince garlic. Cook onion in oil over medium heat until soft, about 2 minutes. Add the garlic and cook for one more minute. Squeeze in the juice from the lemon. Stir in tomato sauce, Tabasco and salt.
Cook for 5 minutes. Remove wing tips and cut wings in half at the joint. Heat oil for deep frying to 375oF.
Cook wings in hot oil until brown, about 8 minutes.
Toss wings in tomato mixture. Serve with chilled celery sticks and blue cheese dressing.

BUFFALO CHICKEN WINGS #5

½ cup	Miracle Whip
¼ cup	Sour Cream
¼ pound	Blue Cheese
4	Ribs Celery
1	Small Onion
2	Cloves Garlic
1 tablespoon	Oil
½	Lemon
8 ounces	Tomato Sauce
¼ cup	Tabasco Sauce
½ teaspoon	Salt
3 pounds	Chicken Wings
	Oil For Frying

Combine Miracle Whip and sour cream. Crumble and stir in the blue cheese. Cut the celery into sticks. Chop onion and mince garlic. Cook onion in oil over medium heat until soft, about 2 minutes. Add the garlic and cook for one more minute. Squeeze in the juice from the lemon. Stir in tomato sauce, Tabasco and salt.
Cook for 5 minutes. Remove wing tips and cut wings in half at the joint. Heat oil for deep frying to 375oF.
Cook wings in hot oil until brown, about 8 minutes.
Toss wings in tomato mixture. Serve with chilled celery sticks and blue cheese dressing.

BUFFALO CHICKEN WINGS #6

2 pounds	Chicken Wings
	Tabasco Sauce
¼ pound	Butter
	Blue Cheese Dressing
	Chilled Celery Sticks
	Chilled Carrot Sticks

Remove tips from wings. Cut wings in half at the joint. Deep-fry in hot oil until golden, about 5 minutes or bake the wings in a 375oF oven for 30-40 minutes until browned. Melt butter and combine with Tabasco Sauce. Add whatever quantity of Tabasco Sauce suits your HOT Button. Coat the wings with the HOT Butter mixture and serve with blue cheese dressing and chilled celery and carrot sticks.

BUFFALO CHICKEN WINGS W/ BLUE CHEESE DIPPING SAUCE

6 tablespoons	Butter or margarine
¼ cup	Hot pepper sauce
	Vegetable oil for frying
18	Chicken wings, disjointed -- tips discarded

Dipping Sauce:

¼ pound	Blue cheese -- Roquefort or
½ cup	Mayonnaise
½ cup	Sour cream
1 tablespoon	Lemon juice
1 tablespoon	Wine vinegar

hot pepper sauce to taste

Prep: 10 minutes Cook: 35 minutes Serves: 36 mini-drumsticks

These spicy hot wings w/ cool, creamy dip are all the rage. Serve w/ plenty of ice-cold beer.

1. Melt butter in a small saucepan. Add hot sauce & remove from the heat.

2. In large frying pan or deep-fat fryer, heat 1" of oil to 375ø. Fry wings in batches w/o crowding until golden brown, 12 1/2 minutes. Drain on paper towels.

3. Brush wings w/ spicy butter & serve warm w/ Blue Cheese dipping sauce.

BLUE CHEESE DIPPING SAUCE
In small bowl, mash the blue cheese, leaving some small lumps. Whisk in the mayonnaise until blended. Add the remaining ingredients & whisk to blend well. Cover & refrigerate until serving time.

BUFFALO CHICKEN WINGS WITH BLUE CHEESE DIPPING SAUCE 2

-----CHICKEN WINGS-----

6 tablespoons	Butter
¼ cup	Hot pepper sauce
	Vegetable oil -- for frying
18	Chicken wings (about 3lb) -- disjointed with tips

-----BLUE CHEESE DIPPING SAUCE-----

1/4 pound	Blue cheese -- roquefort or
½ cup	Mayonnaise
½ cup	Sour cream
1 tablespoon	Lemon juice
1 tablespoon	Wine vinegar

ds Hot pepper sauce

1. Melt butter in a small saucepan. Add hot sauce and remove from heat.

2. In large frying pan or deep-fat fryer, heat 1 inch of oil to 375F. Fry wings in batches without crowding until golden brown, 10 to 15 minutes.
Drain on paper towels.

3. Brush wings with spicy butter and serve warm, with blue cheese dipping sauce.

Sauce:

In a small bowl, mash the blue cheese, leaving some clumps. Whisk in the mayonnaise until blended. Add remaining ingredients and whisk to blend well. Cover and refrigerate until serving time.

Buffalo Wings, from Buffalo N.Y.

4 pounds	Chicken wings
3 tablespoons	Butter -- melted
3 tablespoons	Worcestershire sauce
2 teaspoons	Catsup
2	Garlic cloves -- mashed

-----DIP-----
2/3 cup	Mayonnaise
1/3 cup	Sour cream
1/3 cup	Gorgonzola OR bleu cheese
½ teaspoon	Tabasco
	Celery stalks

Cut off tip of wing. Separate at joint. Place on wire rack in roasting pan. Roast at 350 deg. for 1 1/2 hours. Turn once during cooking.   Combine melted butter, Tabasco, Worcestershire, catsup, garlic and mix well in large bowl. Place chicken in bowl and mix well. Crumble cheese coarsely and mix with other dip ingredients in separate bowl and serve with celery stalks and wings.

CAJUN CHICKEN WINGS

2 ½ pounds	Chicken wings -- separated an
¾ cup	Plain yogurt
2/3 cup	Louisiana hot sauce.
2 teaspoons	Garlic powder
1 cup	Flour
½ cup	Cajun seasoning
	Oil -- for frying

In a bowl, mix together yogurt, hot sauce and garlic. Add chicken and marinate overnight in the refrigerator. The following day, mix together flour and cajun seasonings in a bowl. Remove chicken from the marinade and coat evenly in flour mixture. In a wok or deep fryer, heat oil to 370F.
This can be achieved by heating over medium high heat. Use enough oil to cover 4 to 5 chicken wings at a time. Deep fry wings for approximately 8 minutes. Drain on paper towel. Serves 2 to 4

CAMPBELL'S HONEY MUSTARD WINGS

1 pound	Campbell's dry onion with chives Soup and recipe mix -- dry
½ cup	Honey
¼ cup	Spicy brown mustard
16	Chicken wings -- whole or cut
	Season-all -- to taste

1. In a large bowl, combine soup mix, honey, and mustard. Set aside.

2. Cut wings at joints and discard the tips, or leave the wings whole. Add chicken to soup mixture. Toss to coat.

3. Place chicken in a baking pan greased with Pam spray. Sprinkle with Season-All. Bake at 375 degrees F for about 1 hour or until chicken is don turning once if desired. If wings are getting too brown too soon, cover with tin foil during the latter part of baking time.

Can't Get Enough Chicken Wings

12	chicken wings (2 lbs.)
½ cup	margarine or butter -- melted
1 envelope	Lipton recipe secrets savory herb with garlic recipe soup mix
1 teaspoon	cayenne pepper sauce -- opt'l to taste

Cut tips off chicken wings (save tips for soup.) Cut chicken wings in half at joint. Deep fry, bake or broil until golden brown and crunchy. In medium bowl, blend margarine, savory herb with garlic recipe soup mix and cayenne pepper sauce. Add more or less cayenne pepper to match your 'hot &
spicy tolerance level. Add chicken wings; toss until coated. Serve over greens with cut-up celery, if desired. Makes 24 appetizers.

Chapter 7:

Frozen Desert Recipes

Some of the other Ice cream recipes use these recipes:

Simple Syrup:
4 cups sugar
4 cups water
Place the water and sugar in a saucepan and simmer until the sugar is dissolved. Cool to room temperature, then
refrigerate in a covered jar.
Makes about 1 quart

Custard Ice Cream Base:
This base will keep for 3 to 4 days in the refrigerator in a tightly-covered jar. It is important that the jar be well sealed or the base will pick up flavors from other foods. If you prefer to use turbinado sugar, substitute it for the granulated in the recipe.
1 cup whole milk
3/4 cup sugar
4 egg yolks
3 cups heavy cream
Heat the cream, milk and sugar in a heavy-bottomed saucepan, stirring occasionally until the sugar is dissolved and the mixture is hot. Place the egg yolks in a bowl and whisk briefly. Still whisking, slowly pour in about 1 cup of the hot liquid. When the mixture is smooth, slowly pour it into the liquid in the saucepan, whisking constantly. Cook over medium heat, stirring constantly, until the mixture thickens slightly and coats the back of a spoon, about 8 minutes. Be sure not let the mixture boil at any time or will curdle. Strain into a clean bowl and use as directed in the specific recipes. Stir in the nuts.
Makes 1 quart.

BANANA WALNUT

1 cup milk
2 eggs
1/3 cup sugar
2 bananas, mashed
1 cup cream
1/2 cup walnut pieces

Beat eggs in a bowl. Beat in sugar. Heat milk to almost boiling. Stir into eggs. Stir milk/egg mixture into bananas. Cool. Add cream. Mix in machine. Add walnuts shortly before done.

BERRY, BERRY STRAWBERRY

This is best made with fresh strawberries in season. Of course, that means you can only enjoy for a few weeks in the late spring, then you have to wait a whole year. It's worth the wait.
Take two pints of fresh, ripe strawberries, and prepare them by cleaning and topping them and cutting them into medium sized pieces. Then add in 1/2 cup of sugar and the juice of 1/2 lemon. Let them sit in the refrigerator overnight and then when the ice cream mix (see Old Time Vanilla recipe) has been prepared and aged (chilled in the refrigerator for four hours), add the juice from the strawberry preparation to the mix along with 10 drops of red food coloring and place the remaining strawberries in the freezer compartment of your refrigerator while you
freeze the mix according to the manufacturer s directions. When the ice cream is almost frozen, add in the strawberries and finish freezing.

BLUEBERRY version 1

2 pints blueberries
1 1/2 cups sugar
3 tablespoons orange juice
4 cups light cream
1 teaspoon vanilla extract

In a 3-quart saucepan combines blueberries, sugar and orange juice. Mash berries slightly and cook over medium heat, stirring occasionally, until the mixture comes to a boil. Simmer 5 minutes.
Remove from heat and puree in a food processor or blender. Push mixture through a strainer with the back of a wooden spoon. Cool the mixture. In the chilled canister of ice-cream maker combine blueberry mixture, cream and vanilla. Freeze according to manufacturer's directions.

BLUEBERRY version 2

3 cups blueberries
3 cups table cream
1 1/4 cups sugar

Blend in blender just before putting in machine.
Simple recipe, great ice cream. Nice texture, nice flavor (not too sweet).

BROWN SUGAR PECAN

1 cup milk
1 scant packed cup brown sugar
4 egg yolks
3 cups heavy cream
1 cup pecan pieces

Heat the cream. milk and sugar in a heavy-bottomed saucepan, stirring occasionally until the sugar is dissolved and the mixture is hot. place the egg yolks in a bowl and whisk briefly. Still whisking, slowly pour in about 1 cup of the hot liquid. When the mixture is blended, slowly pour it into the liquid in the saucepan, whisking constantly. Cook over heat, stirring constantly until the mixture thickens slightly and coats the back of a spoon, about 8 minutes. Be sure not let the mixture boil at any time or will curdle. strain into a clean bowl and cool thoroughly. Stir in the nuts.
Pour the mixture into the bowl of the machine and freeze.
Makes 5 cups.

BURNT CARAMEL

(Yields: 1 Quart or 950 ml)
1 C (190 g) granulated sugar
1 C (240 ml) HOT water
4 eggs
1/2 C (40g) powdered sugar
2 C (450 ml) heavy cream
1 tsp vanilla extract

Heat granulated sugar and 1/4 C (60 ml) of the water in a large skillet on medium high heat until the sugar melts and boils, stirring occasionally. Boil until mixture is a dark brown; remove from heat. Gradually stir in remaining 3/4 C (180 ml) water. (I love this part, cause the syrup boils up when the hot water is added) Cool to room temperature and set aside. Beat eggs in a medium bowl until thick and lemon colored; gradually beat in powdered sugar. Stir in cream and vanilla; stir in the caramel mixture. Chill. Freeze in an ice cream machine according to manufacturer's directions.

BUTTER PECAN

2 cups light cream
1 cup brown sugar
2 tablespoons butter
2 cups heavy cream
1 teaspoon vanilla extract
1/2 cup toasted chopped pecans

Combine the light cream, sugar, and butter in a medium saucepan. Cook, stirring constantly over low heat until bubbles form around the edges of the pan. Let the mixture cool and put it in The ice cream machine. Stir in heavy cream and vanilla. Freeze as directed by your machine's manufacturer. Add pecan after ice cream begins to harden.

CARAMEL

5 large egg yolks
1/6 t. salt
8 t. water
2/3 cup + 4 t. sugar
1 1/2 cups milk
1 1/2 cups heavy whipping cream

Place the egg yolks in a large mixing bowl. Add the salt and whisk until smooth. Set aside. Combine the sugar and water in a heavy-bottomed saucepan large enough to eventually hold the milk and cream. Dissolve the sugar in the water over low heat. This may take a while. An alternative is to use the microwave, and then transfer the sugar solution to a saucepan. Increase to high heat and cook the syrup until it is golden amber colored. While the sugar is carmelizing, scald the milk and cream. As soon as the caramel is a golden-amber color, slowly add the milk and cream, 2 T. at a time. Be very careful, as the mixture will bubble up. Whisk the caramel cream into the eggs. Strain and refrigerate until cold. Freeze according to ice cream machine instructions.

CARAMEL ALMOND

1 cup sugar
1 cup boiling water
4 cups heavy cream
1/2 cup sugar
6 egg yolks, lightly beaten
pinch of salt
1 tsp. vanilla
toasted almonds

In heavy pan, heat 1 cup sugar until it melts and becomes golden in color. CAREFULLY add boiling water to syrup(partially cover pan while doing this so the caramel doesn't splash on you.) Stir until dissolved. Bring to boil and cook until thick(9-10 min.) Set aside. In another pan scald cream. Add sugar and mix well. Pour cream slowly over egg yolks, stirring constantly. Return to saucepan and cook over medium heat, stirring constantly, until thickened. Add salt, vanilla, and 3/4 cups of the caramel syrup(saving the rest.) Mix well. Freeze in ice cream maker according to instructions. Serve topped with remaining caramel syrup and toasted almonds.

CHERRY

3/4 cup dried cherries
1/2 cup rum
2 1/2 cups light cream
1/2 cup sugar
4 egg yolks
1/4 teaspoon vanilla

Place the cherries in a bowl and cover with rum. Allow to soak for several hours or overnight.
Heat the light cream and sugar together until the sugar is dissolved and bubbles begin to form around edge of the pot. Whisk yolks until creamy. Add 1/2 cup of the warm cream to the egg yolks. Pour the warmed yolks back into the half-and-half and continue to cook, stirring, until the custard mixture coats the back of a spoon. Do not boil the mixture or it will curdle. Stir in the vanilla, allow to cool completely, then chill. Pour into the ice-cream maker and freeze according to manufacturer's directions. Drain the cherries. When the mixture begins to thicken as it freezes, add the cherries and freeze until ice cream is the proper consistency.

CHERRY BERRY

2 Env unflavored gelatin
1 1/2 c Sugar
1/2 c Water
10 oz Frozen sliced strawberries
2 c Dark sweet cherries
4 c Light cream or half & half
2 c Whipping cream
2 ts Vanilla

In a small saucepan combine unflavored gelatin and sugar. Add water and strawberries. Cook over medium heat, stirring constantly, until mixture just comes to a boil. Remove from heat and cool to room temperature. Meanwhile, chop cherries. In a 3 quart or larger ice cream freezer combine half and half, whipping cream, vanilla, strawberry mixture and cherries. Freeze according to manufacturer's direction or place in freezer containers and freeze at least 4 hours. Makes about 3 quarts.

CHOCOLATE version 1

4 egg yolks, lightly beaten
1 cup sugar
2 cups table cream (18% milk fat)
1 1/2 cups milk
1/2 cup cocoa powder (sifted)
2 tsp pure vanilla extract

Beat egg yolks lightly. Beat in sugar. Heat the cream/milk on the stove. As it's heating, beat in cocoa powder. Heat cream/milk/cocoa mix until steaming. Stir into egg/sugar mix. Add vanilla extract. Cool. Freeze in ice cream maker.
Notes:
I use Dutch processed cocoa (instead of American processed), but I'm not sure how much difference it makes. I've tried using a higher milk fat content, but then the mix takes on the consistency of pudding when cooled, and doesn't freeze hard enough in ice cream maker.

CHOCOLATE version 2

4 oz unsweetened chocolate (I used Ghirardelli)
1 1/4 cup milk
2 eggs, lightly beaten
1 cup sugar
1 cup cream
1 pinch salt
1 tsp pure vanilla extract
1/2 cup milk

Melt chocolate over low heat while heating milk over low heat. Gradually stir milk into melted chocolate. If you don't stir milk in gradually, chocolate will clump and you will have difficulty breaking it down. If you stir milk in gradually, chocolate will clump, but you'll be able to break it down when you add a little more milk. Heat while stirring until smooth. Mixture will become thick. Beat sugar into eggs. Stir in hot chocolate/milk mixture into eggs. Add cream, salt, vanilla, and extra 1/2 cup milk. Cool. Freeze in ice cream maker.

CHOCOLATE version 3

3 eggs
1/2 cup sugar
8 oz bittersweet chocolate
1 cup milk
2 cups table cream (18% milk fat)
1 tablespoon cocoa powder
1 tablespoon vanilla extract
Beat eggs lightly. Beat sugar into eggs. Heat chocolate, milk, and 1 cup of cream together in a sauce pan. Stir occasionally until chocolate starts to melt. When chocolate partially melted, stir in cocoa powder. When hot (and chocolate fully melted and cocoa dissolved) but not boiling, remove from stove and stir in to eggs. Add second cup of cream and vanilla. Cool. and make in ice cream maker.

CHOCOLATE ALMOND

Chocolate Ice Cream mix (see recipe)
3/4 cup toasted almonds
Make a batch of chocolate ice cream (see recipe). When nearly frozen, add the toasted almonds.
Note: You will obtain better results if you toast your own almonds. Buy blanched almonds, toast in the oven at 250 for 2-4 minutes (watch them carefully so they don't burn). You may want to chop the almonds before toasting if you prefer smaller pieces.

CHOCOLATE ALMOND BUTTER

2 oz bittersweet chocolate
5 Tbl cocoa powder
2 cup milk
3 eggs, lightly beaten
1 cup sugar
1 cup cream
1.5 tsp pure vanilla extract
3/4 cup almond butter

Melt chocolate over low heat.
Gradually stir in cocoa powder and milk while continuing to heat. You want the consistency to be thick but not solid as you add the milk and cocoa powder. Beat sugar into eggs. Stir hot chocolate/milk mixture into eggs. Add cream and vanilla extract. Cool. Just before adding to ice cream maker, stir a cup of ice cream mixture into almond butter. Once mixed, stir into rest of ice cream mixture. Freeze in ice cream maker according to manufacturer's instructions.

CHOCOLATE BANANA

3 eggs
1 cup sugar
2 oz bittersweet chocolate
2 cups table cream (18% milkfat)
1 1/2 cups milk
6 tablespoons cocoa powder
1 tablespoon vanilla extract
3 over-ripe bananas
Juice of 1 lemon
Beat eggs lightly
Beat sugar in to eggs
Melt chocolate in milk and cream
When chocolate partially melted, stir in cocoa powder.
Continue stirring chocolate/cream mixture until hot but not quite boiling
Stir hot chocolate/cream mixture in to eggs.
Stir in vanilla extract.
Cool.
When ready to make, mash bananas and lemon juice together
Make chocolate mixture in ice cream maker.
Just before ready, add banana mixture.
Note: Use good quality, *very* ripe bananas. Otherwise your ice cream will have a strange flavor.

www.ingramcontent.com/pod-product-compliance
Lightning Source LLC
Chambersburg PA
CBHW081625100526

44590CB00021B/3610